**New Directions for
Teaching and Learning**

Marilla D. Svinicki
EDITOR-IN-CHIEF

D0987371

2

·158

2009

700201

000

Internationalizing the Curriculum in Higher Education

Carolin Kreber
EDITOR

Number 118 • Summer 2009
Jossey-Bass
San Francisco

INTERNATIONALIZING THE CURRICULUM IN HIGHER EDUCATION
Carolin Kreber (ed.)
New Directions for Teaching and Learning, no. 118
Marilla D. Svinicki, Editor-in-Chief

Microfilm copies of issues and articles are available in 16mm and 35mm, as well as microfiche in 105mm, through University Microfilms, Inc., 300 North Zeeb Road, Ann Arbor, Michigan 48106-1346.

NEW DIRECTIONS FOR TEACHING AND LEARNING (ISSN 0271-0633, electronic ISSN 1536-0768) is part of The Jossey-Bass Higher and Adult Education Series and is published quarterly by Wiley Subscription Services, Inc., A Wiley Company, at Jossey-Bass, 989 Market Street, San Francisco, California 94103-1741. Periodicals postage paid at San Francisco, California, and at additional mailing offices. POSTMASTER: Send address changes to New Directions for Teaching and Learning, Jossey-Bass, 989 Market Street, San Francisco, California 94103-1741.

New Directions for Teaching and Learning is indexed in CIJE: Current Index to Journals in Education (ERIC), Contents Pages in Education (T&F), Current Abstracts (EBSCO), Educational Research Abstracts Online (T&F), ERIC Database (Education Resources Information Center), Higher Education Abstracts (Claremont Graduate University), and SCOPUS (Elsevier).

SUBSCRIPTIONS cost $98 for individuals and $251 for institutions, agencies, and libraries in the United States. Prices subject to change.

EDITORIAL CORRESPONDENCE should be sent to the editor-in-chief, Marilla D. Svinicki, Department of Educational Psychology, University of Texas at Austin, One University Station, D5800, Austin, TX 78712.

www.josseybass.com

CONTENTS

FROM THE SERIES EDITOR

About this Publication

Since 1980, *New Directions for Teaching and Learning* (NDTL) has brought a unique blend of theory, research, and practice to leaders in postsecondary education. *NDTL* sourcebooks strive not only for solid substance but also for timeliness, compactness, and accessibility.

The series has four goals: to inform readers about current and future directions in teaching and learning in postsecondary education, to illuminate the context that shapes these new directions, to illustrate these new directions through examples from real settings, and to propose ways in which these new directions can be incorporated into still other settings.

This publication reflects the view that teaching deserves respect as a high form of scholarship. We believe that significant scholarship is conducted not only by researchers who report results of empirical investigations, but also by practitioners who share disciplines reflections about teaching. Contributors to *NDTL* approach questions of teaching and learning as seriously as they approach substantive questions in their own disciplines, and they deal not only with pedagogical issues but also with the intellectual and social context in which these issues arise. Authors deal on the one hand with theory and research and on the other with practice, and they translate from research and theory to practice and back again.

About this Volume

The world is growing smaller and smaller as our capacities to communicate grow larger and larger. It is imperative that our institutions prepare our students to live in this global community. The current issue provides some thoughts about how this can be done.

Marilla D. Svinicki
Editor-in-Chief

Marilla D. Svinicki is the director of the Center for Teaching Effectiveness at the University of Texas at Austin.

Although internationalization efforts in higher education have become increasingly driven by economic considerations, this is not the case for all initiatives, particularly those at the level of curriculum, where academic, social/cultural, ethical, political, and even environmental rationales feature more strongly.

Different Perspectives on Internationalization in Higher Education

Carolin Kreber

Faculty, administrators, students, policy makers and the larger community committed to internationalization must answer several difficult questions. What should the process include? Is reading a few books from different cultures enough to internationalize education?

Murphy, 2007, p. 181

"Internationalization" has become a key theme and widespread phenomenon in higher education. In this introduction, I explore different meanings and motivations underlying the notion of internationalization in higher education, thereby providing a richer conceptual basis from which to appreciate efforts directed at internationalizing the curriculum in particular. In the final section, I provide an overview of the examples featured in this volume.

Internationalization in the Context of Globalization

Given that higher education takes place within a globalizing world (Enders and Fulton, 2002), internationalization and globalization are often discussed together; however, although related, it is useful to distinguish the two

NEW DIRECTIONS FOR TEACHING AND LEARNING, no. 118, Summer 2009 © Wiley Periodicals, Inc.
Published online in Wiley InterScience (www.interscience.wiley.com) • DOI: 10.1002/tl.348

phenomena. In the first part of this chapter, I draw on some of the policy literature on internationalization in higher education, as discussions about how to internationalize the curriculum in particular are usefully enriched by placing them within this larger context.

Many analysts consider internationalization efforts to be countries' or institutions' proactive responses to the external macro socioeconomic processes and effects of globalization over which they have no control (e.g., Knight, 1997; Van der Wende, 1997, 1999). In Knight's (1997) own words:

> Globalization is the flow of technology, economy, knowledge, people, values, ideas . . . across borders. Globalization affects each country in a different way due to a nation's individual history, traditions, culture and priorities. Internationalization of higher education is one of the ways a country responds to the impact of globalization yet, at the same time respects the individuality of the nation (p. 6).

According to Van der Wende (1996), internationalization refers to "any systematic, sustained effort aimed at making higher education (more) responsive to the requirements and challenges related to the globalization of societies, economy and labour markets" (p. 23).

Commenting on the role of nation states under either condition (that of globalization or that of internationalization), Enders and Fulton (2002) similarly argue that globalization refers principally to increased interdependence and, eventually, convergence of markets, cultures, and societies where individual states are seen to have little power. Internationalization, on the other hand, describes greater mutual cooperation between states and activity across state borders. Globalization challenges the power of the nation state; internationalization assumes that states still play a crucial role. According to this perspective then, globalization is primarily associated with increased interdependence and convergence and an ethos of competition, while internationalization tends to be associated principally with an ethos of mutuality and practices geared at strengthening cooperation. However, how people understand the idea of internationalizing higher education varies greatly, further serving as evidence that it does not represent a unidimensional concept.

According to Vught and colleagues, internationalization in higher education is seen to include several activities and processes such as:

> The transnational mobility of students and staff, internationalization of curricula and quality assurance, interinstitutional cooperation in education and research, and the establishment of international university consortia. Furthermore, there has been strong growth in the cross-border delivery of education, leading to a substantial market in export and import of higher education products and services (Van Vught, Van der Wende, and Westerhejden, 2002, p. 103).

NEW DIRECTIONS FOR TEACHING AND LEARNING • DOI: 10.1002/tl

The motivation for increased cross-border delivery of education can be explained in two ways. On the one hand, there is now a much greater market for higher education, particularly in countries with less well-developed higher education systems. As well, it is through cooperating with institutions in other countries, and the sharing of resources this implies, that teaching and research programs can be enriched and in some cases become affordable to the institution. This cooperation can be observed not only between developed, or developed and developing countries, but also between developing countries (Murphy, 2007, for example discusses cooperation efforts between a Mexican institution and one in Eastern Europe). On the other hand, universities in Western countries see this increased demand for higher education, particularly in so-called developing countries, as a very welcome opportunity to boost their budgets, which, coinciding with deregulation in many jurisdictions, have experienced substantial declines in public contributions over the past decade. These institutions then compete with other providers for what they perceive to be lucrative cross-border opportunities.

I should note, albeit briefly, that numerous observers predict that the pressures many countries experience with regard to international competition will expand drastically through initiatives by the World Trade Organization (WTO), particularly the highly contested General Agreement on Trade in Services (GATS). GATS considers higher education as a trade-related sector and legalizes the cross-border/global trade in educational services (e.g., Van Vught et al., 2002). Stromquist (2007) and Van Vught et al. (2002) report that education and training represents the fifth largest service sector in the United States, explaining the strong interest of the United States (but also, e.g., Australia, the United Kingdom, and New Zealand), in supporting the liberalization of free trade of higher education across borders.

Exploring Different Motivations for Internationalization

Following Knight (1997), Qiang (2003) provides a useful conceptual framework of four different possible rationales for internationalization in higher education: the political, the academic, the cultural/social, and the economic. The political rationale is principally related to issues of national security, stability, and peace as well as ideological influences ensuing from internationalization efforts. The academic rationale is principally linked to the goal of achieving international standards for both teaching and research. More generally, the reasoning goes that by encouraging greater internationalization across teaching, research, and service activities, the quality of higher education can be enriched. The cultural/social rationale is based on the view that the "homogenizing effects of globalization" (Knight, 1997, p. 11) need to be resisted and the culture as well as language of nations be respected. This view places particular emphasis on understanding foreign languages and cultures, the preservation of national culture, and respect for diversity. Finally, there is the economic rationale, which, by many, is considered to be a direct response to the market forces associated with the economic dimension of globalization. On the one hand, the economic rationale underlies efforts aimed at developing the human resources/capital needed for the nation to stay internationally competitive; on the other hand, it underlies efforts geared towards increasing the institution's (or sector's) income by providing education abroad or attracting more foreign students.

Although until the 1990s internationalization in higher education was largely understood to be a cooperative effort with its rationale based primarily on political, cultural, and academic arguments, many observers today feel that internationalization has become increasingly economically motivated (e.g., Kälvermark and Van der Wende, 1997; Van der Wende, 2001; see also Grabove in this volume). While the political, cultural, and academic rationales are based on an ethos of cooperation, the economic one is based on an ethos of competition. Surely, both these overarching rationales—cooperation across state borders and competition—can be observed in contemporary efforts to internationalize higher education but it is the latter which is more and more seen to dominate the internationalization agenda.

Relatedly, it has been proposed that it might be useful to distinguish between "internationalization" and "internationalism" (Stromquist, 2007; Jones, 2000), as they are informed by different considerations. According to this framework, internationalism emphasizes notions such as "international community, international cooperation, international community of interests, and international dimensions of the common good" (Jones, 2000, p. 31). Internationalization, on the other hand, is seen to refer to "greater international presence by the dominant economic and political powers, usually guided by principles of marketing and competition" (Stromquist, 2007, p. 82). Stromquist concludes that internationalization in higher education is therefore closely associated with the "entrepreneurialism" or "academic capitalism" that Slaughter (1998) and colleagues observed among universities in the 1990s (in the United States, Australia, Canada, and the United Kingdom) as these were competing for external funds.

If one were to adopt these definitions of internationalism and internationalization, a concern over internationalism could be observed among scholars who call for the raising of intercultural awareness and development of global citizenship through schools and colleges (e.g., Ladson-Billings, 2005; Nussbaum, 1997; see also several contributors to this volume). Then again, as we saw in the earlier discussion of the cultural and political rationales underlying internationalization efforts, the term "internationalization" can be interpreted to include "internationalism" as well. Murphy (2007), for example, suggests that "Internationalization of education is seen as one way to bridge the gap between developing and developed countries and as a strategy for the formation of citizens adept at and functioning in a multicultural global system" (p. 198).

NEW DIRECTIONS FOR TEACHING AND LEARNING • DOI: 10.1002/tl

What can we conclude from this? Surely, the actual terms we employ to describe our "cross-border" activities and policies ("internationalism" versus "internationalization") are perhaps less critical; what is very important, however, is to be clear about the assumptions and motivations driving our efforts.

Further Considerations Regarding these Varied Rationales

What are some of the implications of all this? I would suggest that one fundamental problem with the economic rationale (i.e., efforts aimed at developing the human resources needed for the nation to stay internationally competitive and/or efforts geared towards generating income by providing education abroad or attracting more foreign students) is that it can all too easily become the principal driver in how the purposes of higher education become defined.

To begin with, and to link this wider discussion more explicitly to the notion of "curriculum," I should note that I see a real risk for curricula now being superficially internationalized in response to such economic imperatives so as to make them more appealing to international students, which, in turn, would mean that more international students come to study with us (and with that, more cash in our institution's pocket). If internationalizing the curriculum is not understood to serve a more profound educational purpose, one that—while inclusive of aims to meet the needs of international students—goes well beyond this, then an important opportunity for higher education to play a pivotal role in fostering intercultural understanding, greater empathy and action towards those most in need, international cooperation on climate change, etc., is lost. More on that later.

There is a more general concern as well. In a globalized market economy, nation-states compete with one another within the same market for the same resources. In such a market, what counts is no longer so much that the provider (for example, your university or college or mine) is confident that we offer sound or "high quality" programs, but instead how the worth of the program is perceived by the "consumer" and whether the programs (in their form of delivery and curriculum content) are judged as being relevant to consumer needs or the economy. Hence, institutions are progressively more called upon to offer programs that potential clients will consider valuable, which more often than not, means "useful" for the economy and career advancement. At the same time, we observe greater obsession with quality assurance. In such a context, the very meaning of the "quality of education" and how to determine it becomes more contested than ever. Quality is intrinsically connected to purposes (indeed, we think of something that is of high quality as being fit for purpose), yet the purposes of higher education have become increasingly diverse and conflicting (Barnett, 1992; Rowland, 2006), in no small part as a result of the economic dimension of globalization. It is in this spirit that some observers (e.g., Kivinen, 2002; Newman, 2000) caution that concern with global competitiveness could lead higher education to easily lose sight of its traditional academic values such as social criticism, preparation for civic life, and the pursuit of curiosity-driven learning and scholarship.

Now, having voiced these concerns over economically driven internationalization initiatives, some qualifying remarks are required. I think Knight (1997) is absolutely right to emphasize that the impact of globalization, and hence internationalization efforts, will be perceived differently depending on how a particular country is positioned within the global society/economy. Moreover, there are positive, even ethically defendable outcomes to partially, or even entirely, economically motivated efforts to increase internationalization. Strengthening the economy and addressing other development needs of developing countries, through their internationalization efforts (which can take on many different forms including sending students abroad and inviting foreign resources), is clearly important but has different consequences for the country that is "providing services" and the country that is "receiving" them. A real problem arises when economically motivated efforts become the overriding concerns for education, and particularly, if in a free market, countries most in need of development remain the most disadvantaged as a result of unequal opportunity. Murphy (2007) adds three further possible and interrelated risks to developing countries that see internationalization as a solution to their development needs: the imposition of foreign and inadequate models to solve domestic problems, the potential loss of human and intellectual capital, and connected to the previous two, the weakening of the domestic university system as it plays a marginal role in the development of the country.

Interest in internationalization has increased drastically since the 1990s. Many critics suggest that this is principally a result of economic considerations and perceptions of external pressure. However, although this is perhaps the case at the level of wider national and institutional policies directed at providing services abroad, recruiting foreign students, and stressing the employability of graduates, the motivation driving many individual faculty, or groups of faculty, to making changes to individual courses or programs lies elsewhere. As David Kahane argues in Chapter Five, "For many educators, . . . a key reason for internationalization is ethical: It helps students to examine their implicit and explicit beliefs about whose wellbeing matters, and to develop a more globalized sense of responsibility and citizenship."

One might suggest that the humanitarian crises in many parts of the world have given rise to internationalization efforts through education in developed countries that have as their goal to enhance international awareness, empathy and social action among staff, students and hence, future (world) leaders, and are motivated by cultural/social, political, and ethical rationales. To address the development needs identified by certain communities some institutions (or countries) decide to offer their (educational) services. Such efforts are perhaps, or in all probability, also economically motivated. However, the extent to which economic reasons are dominant rather than intermingled with, or in many instances secondary to, social or humanitarian considerations will vary from case to case. Then again, reasons to enhance efforts directed at internationalization might lie elsewhere altogether. One might argue, for example, that the events following September 11, 2001, or concern over sustainable development and the survival of our planet, will have spurred further national interest in international cooperation as well as in policies and activities linked to the political, cultural/ social and environmental rationales of internationalization.

Scope of Meaning and Perceived Outcomes of Internationalization Efforts

The Scope of Meaning of Internationalization. As has become evident already, people understand different things by internationalization. For some, for example, internationalizing higher education has been taken to mean integrating international content or perspectives in each of the academic disciplines. The reasoning behind this view is that it is through exposure to these international perspectives, and a better understanding of the international circumstances of other people or cultures, that students are adequately prepared for the world in which they are living (Groennings and Wiley, 1990). Since the 1980s, universities had witnessed greater interest in international education programs, as indicated by curricula taking up international subjects, incorporating international comparative approaches, and increasing their offerings of international areas studies. However, it is particularly since the 1990s that internationalization is seen to be relevant across traditional programs or disciplines.

Echvin and Ray (2002) as well as Thune and Welle-Strand (2005) suggest that efforts directed at internationalization at program level can be observed by the contribution of one or more of the following four factors:

- The recruitment of international students
- The teaching process, through selection of particular course content and forms of delivery (including ICT), student mobility, language of instruction, etc.
- Resources—in the form of internationally recruited staff members, use of international course materials (e.g., literature), etc.
- Location—offering courses or setting up campuses abroad

Taking an even broader lens on internationalization, Knight (1993) argued that internationalization of higher education refers to "the process of integrating an international/intercultural dimension into the teaching, research and service functions of the institution" (p. 21). Qiang (2003), echoing the notion of integration inherent in Knight's definition, concludes that "internationalization must be *entrenched* (emphasis added) in the culture, policy, planning and organizational process of the institution so that it can be both successful and sustainable" (p. 258). Yet, studies show that the extent to which administrators and faculty at colleges and universities engage with calls to further their internationalization efforts is not the least a measure of how relevant they consider internationalization to be to their particular field (Schoorinan, 1999).

Does studying in internationalized contexts make a difference? Murphy (2007) discussed the extent to which internationalized campuses or programs make a difference and cited a number of studies that attest to the positive effects of internationalization efforts on students. Based on these studies, she reports that governments and universities hold the view that students who study on internationalized campuses demonstrate greater knowledge of international events, perspectives, and methods. She further observes that these students are seen to be better prepared to contribute positively to local, regional, national, and international progress because they develop skills deemed necessary for the modern workforce and global conditions, such as second-language acquisition, cultural awareness, international contacts, and adaptation skills (p. 173).

She also reports on studies that show that students themselves perceive an internationalized education to be beneficial for personal and career development. Although all these studies are very encouraging, Qiang (2003) cautions that further research is needed "to identify those competencies which help students to be successful national and international citizens and to contribute to local and global work environments" (p. 250).

Why another volume on internationalization? Internationalization is an important policy issue in higher education; yet, what precisely internationalization means with regards to teaching and learning, and what it can add to the student learning experience, is far less often talked or written about. As Van Gyn and her colleagues argue in Chapter Three, "the concept of internationalization and its contribution to higher education is inadequately understood by most" and "getting to the heart of what internationalization means in higher education is not a simple matter."

Key questions this volume addresses are "What do we understand by integrating an international dimension in education?" "Why do we think doing so is important? And how far have we come? "What are some internationalization initiatives that can be observed on our own campuses?" Rather than asking contributors to provide comprehensive case studies of how their institution attempts to integrate an international dimension into its teaching (and research and service functions), which would have been a rather onerous task, I invited them to share their experiences of trying to work towards internationalizing education within their own personal and clearly demarcated contexts. As was suggested by Van Vught and colleagues (2002) earlier, "internationalization of the curriculum" is but one of a range of possible activities underlying internationalization efforts. So what is meant, in this volume, by "curriculum"?

For me, the curriculum includes the rather narrow definition of the individual courses or programs offered by our colleges and universities; however, I do mean more by it. By "curriculum," I mean all the activities, experiences, and learning opportunities (that is, the entire teaching and learning environment) that students, academics, administrators, and support staff are part of. The curriculum involves the entire institution and all the intended (and unintended) messages conveyed to students while they are studying in our programs and on our campuses. In discussing examples of internationalizing the curriculum, most contributors to this volume take the approach of a particular course or program they were responsible for. Others look at their institution more broadly.

As will become clear in the chapters that follow, none of the contributors felt that "reading a few books from different cultures (was) enough to internationalize education" (Murphy, 2007, p. 181), and all had to think carefully about "What should the process include" (Murphy, 2007, p. 181). However, none suggested that the processes and activities underlying their initiative portrayed a perfect account of an internationalized curriculum. The value of these chapters lies in the varied interpretations they offer on what internationalizing the curriculum might involve and also in the concrete illustrations they provide of what each of us could do, in our own backyards, as it were, to make the higher education experience more internationally inclusive and/or relevant. Some of the examples featured here go beyond the traditional discourse of internationalization. This is deliberate, as my intent is also to broaden this discourse and give these conceptions and practices a "voice" within it. Indeed, they enrich our understanding of internationalization in very useful ways.

My purpose with this volume is to engender reflection and dialogue within the academy about what internationalizing the curriculum could mean and how the process of internationalizing education might be enhanced. As Qiang (2003), Van der Wende (1996), and Knight (1993) have noted, attempts at internationalization will not be truly successful or sustainable unless they become fully integrated into all the activities and policies of the institution. So ultimately, discussions will need to include policy makers, administrators and those serving on central committees where not only academic regulations (as is typically the case), but also educational purposes as well as pedagogies are routinely discussed. To be clear, internationalization is not just about how and where we deliver our educational services. Reflecting on what internationalization means cannot be separated from critically engaging with the question of what the purposes and goals of higher education should be, within specific programs and across programs, and the role of teachers, students, administrators and the institution as a whole in contributing to these purposes.

In the concluding section, I provide a brief overview of the chapters that follow, drawing appropriately on some of the classification systems introduced earlier.

Internationalizing the Curriculum: Examples Featured in this Volume

In Chapter Two, Valerie L. Grabove describes how a mid-sized community college in Ontario embraces the notion of internationalization. Although her analysis concludes that most of the institutional initiatives are market-driven and aimed at increasing revenue, she also observes that these entrepreneurial efforts at college-level have had the desirable side effect of leading academic staff across the college to become more sensitized to, and educated in, the notion of internationalization. This, in turn, has resulted in gradual changes in programs and curricula. Valerie offers us an excellent example of how economic rationales, although often the trigger for new initiatives, in practice, are often intermingled with academic, social/cultural, and other motivations.

In Chapter Three, Geraldine Van Gyn and her colleagues describe a faculty development initiative at a university in western Canada designed to help academics in remodeling their courses to make them more internationally relevant and sensitive to intercultural issues. The authors make clear that it was very important at the beginning of the initiative to engage in discussion on what "internationalizing curriculum" might/should mean. Together with colleagues from their institution they concluded that internationalizing the curriculum involves "educating for world-mindedness." Educating for world-mindedness comprises more than selecting appropriate contents and pedagogies to ensure that these address the needs of international students; it also implies awareness raising among all students and staff of issues of diversity and intercultural sensitivity and the full integration of these considerations into the curriculum. Thinking about course design through the lens of educating for world-mindedness prompts among many faculty a process of transformation of the assumptions guiding their educational purposes and pedagogies. The rationale underlying this internationalization of curricula is principally social/cultural and academic.

In Chapter Four, Bobbie Turniansky and colleagues also argue that internationalizing higher education does not just involve adding international content. If one of the roles of higher education is to prepare students to survive and thrive in an uncertain, globalized world, faculty and students have to develop a multicultural attitude, one that is sensitive to, and appreciative of, cultural diversity. The key to this, as they suggest, is to explore with students the cultural aspects of their own personal and professional identity. Specifically, they discuss the process and outcomes of a workshop they offer within their culturally diverse teacher education program in Israel. They contend that the principles underlying the workshop hold true for any "people professions," including scientists working in teams, accountants dealing with clients, and historians trying to understand past human events. The rationale underlying this view on internationalizing curriculum is principally social/cultural and possibly political.

David Kahane, in Chapter Five, also suggests that internationalization involves cultivating a meaningful and motivating sense of global citizenship. Drawing on his own experience of teaching undergraduate philosophy, he discusses the limits of both "pedagogies of reason" and "pedagogies of sentiment" in helping us recognize and challenge our own privilege and overcome our dissociation from others' suffering. He highlights instead the pivotal role that "contemplative pedagogies" such as meditation and free writing can play in connecting students more deeply with their own humanity and, by overcoming alienation from their internal worlds, foster a more globalized sense of responsibility and citizenship.

The next chapter, by Martin Haigh, builds nicely on David's ideas. Critical of approaches that treat internationalization as the addition of multicultural elements to a Western curriculum, Martin makes an even more radical proposal. Specifically, he explores the possibility of internationalizing the undergraduate curriculum by organizing it around a non-Western framework rooted in Indian philosophy, thereby lifting, or perhaps rather freeing, internationalization efforts from their Eurocentric foundations. An important aspect of the framework he advocates, which he refers to as a "Sattvic curriculum," is that it promotes self-reflection and self-development among students, thereby having the potential to overcome present barriers to empathy, genuine commitment, and global citizenship. Martin discusses the educational benefits of, and main objections voiced against, such a proposal.

In Chapter Seven, Jean C. Florman and colleagues describe how an existing partnership between two communities, one in eastern Iowa and one in Mexico, was turned into a cross-disciplinary and international service learning course for students in the University of Iowa Colleges of Engineering, Pharmacy, and Liberal Arts and Sciences. The projects that students worked on through the service-learning component of their university courses were directly related to the development needs the Mexican community had identified. Jean and her colleagues discuss the benefits of the initiative for both communities and make suggestions for how it could be enhanced in the future. Analyzing this particular internationalization initiative in terms of its underlying motivation, one might say that the main driver was a willingness to offer voluntary services where they were needed, to use the existing partnership to offer richer learning opportunities within a broad range of disciplines, but also to learn about other cultures. Jean and her colleagues add that the initiative "offered eastern Iowa high school and university students a unique opportunity to provide service in an international setting, gain the deep personal satisfaction that comes from performing service work, and forge permanent international friendships."

In Chapter Eight, Ross A. Perkins reports on a partnership between an institution in Malawi and one in the United States funded by The United States Agency for International Development (USAID). As part of this partnership, lecturers from Mzuzu University in Malawi studied at Virginia Tech on a master's program in instructional technology to acquire the knowledge and skills needed to offer a distance teacher education program back home. The partnership also included the joined redesign of a course to be offered in Malawi. Ross describes how the course was successfully redesigned as a result of an effective collaboration between educators at Mzuzu University in Malawi and Virginia Tech. Looked at through the four-dimensional lens of internationalization at the program level introduced earlier (Echvin and Ray, 2002; Thune and Welle-Strand, 2005), one might observe that the initiative included foreign student recruitment (these students did receive scholarships from Virginia Tech to pay their tuition), the teaching process was adapted by making changes to particular course content and forms of delivery, resources included collaboration with staff from Malawi, and in terms of location, the idea was to set up courses abroad. Yet, the driver for this project was a shortage of teachers in Malawi, a development need identified by the Ministry of Education in Malawi.

In Chapter Nine, Arja Vainio-Mattila reports on an academic course at the undergraduate level ("Think Global–Act Local"), offered in partnership with local NGOs, that raised student awareness of how global problems play themselves out at local levels (here, a mid-sized town in central Ontario). Arja also turns a critical eye on the assumptions that presently guide efforts directed at internationalization and argues for "anchoring the process of internationalization in the core educational mission of higher education rather than presenting it as a delivery mechanism." Drawing on the work of bell hooks and Paulo Freire, she makes a case for embedding internationalization efforts within a critical pedagogy. In essence she proposes to create learning environments that afford students the opportunity to "not only becoming good (read compliant) global citizens but agents of change actively pursuing more equal and just relationships which may or may not be international but are always global."

In Chapter Ten, Tarah S. A. Wright, like Arja, links the internationalization of higher education curricula to a need for universities to grapple with global issues. More specifically, Tarah explores internationalization efforts through the lens of global sustainability and examines the role of universities in educating for sustainable development through their research, their teaching (and pedagogies), and by acting as models in their own physical operations. Rather than suggesting that sustainability should be promoted through specialized courses or programs, she advocates an integrated approach where sustainability is considered across the disciplines. She concludes that "In order for higher education to truly address sustainability problems and educate the citizenry to move toward sustainability, a fundamental re-thinking of the purpose of the university and how we teach is needed."

Final Comment

Universities and colleges are increasingly called upon to internationalize. A comprehensive conception of internationalization can help us resist undue emphasis on economic imperatives on the one hand, and purely cosmetic efforts at internationalizing curriculum on the other, both at the expense of considerations of the common good.

References

Barnett, R. Improving Higher Education. Total Quality Care. Buckingham, UK: SRHE (The Society for Research into Higher Education) and Open University Press, 1992.

Echvin, C., and Ray, D. "Measuring Internationalization in Educational Institutions. Case Study: French Management Schools." Higher Education Management and Policy, 2002, 14(1), 292–296.

Enders, J., and Fulton, O. "Blurring Boundaries and Blistering Institutions." In J. Enders and O. Fulton (eds.), Higher Education in a Globalising World. International Trends and Mutual Observations. A Festschrift in Honour of Ulrich Teichler, 1–17. Dordrecht, The Netherlands: Kluwer Academic Publishers, 2002.

Groennings, S., and Wiley, D. Group Portrait: Internationalizing the Disciplines. The American Forum for Global Education. International Education Series. New York, NY: The American Forum, 1990.

Jones, P. "Globalization and Internationalism: Democratic Prospects for World Education." In N. Stromquist and K. Monkman (eds.), Globalization and Education: Integration and Contestation across Cultures, 27–42. Boulder: Rowmann and Littlefield, 2000.

Kälvermark, T., and Van der Wende, M. C. (eds.) National Policies for Internationalisation of Higher Education in Europe. Stockholm: National Agency for Higher Education, 1997.

Kivinen, O. "Higher Learning in an Age of Uncertainty. A Postmodern Critique to Contemporary University Practices." In J. Enders and O. Fulton (eds.), Higher Education in a Globalising World. International Trends and Mutual Observations. A Festschrift in Honour of Ulrich Teichler, 191–207. Dordrecht, The Netherlands: Kluwer Academic Publishers, 2002.

Knight, J. "Internationalization: Management Strategies and Issues." International Education Magazine, 1993, 9(6), 21–22.

Knight, J. "Internationalisation of Higher Education: A Conceptual Framework." In J. Knight and H. de Wit (eds.), Internationalisation of Higher Education in Asia Pacific Countries, 5–19. Amsterdam: European Association for International Education (EAIE), 1997.

Ladson-Billings, G. "Differing Concepts of Citizenship: Schools and Communities as Cites of Civic Development." In N. Noddings (ed.), Educating Citizens for Global Awareness, 69–80. New York: Teachers College Press, 2005.

Murphy, M. "Experiences in the Internationalization of Education. Strategies to Promote Equality of Opportunity at Monterray Tech." Higher Education, 2007, 53(2), 167–208.

Newman, F. "Saving Higher Education's Soul." Change Magazine of Higher Education, September/October 2000, 2–9.

Nussbaum, M. Cultivating Humanity: A Classical Defense of Reform in Liberal Education. Cambridge, Mass.: Harvard University, Cahners Publishing, 1997.

Qiang, Z. "Internationalization of Higher Education: Towards a Conceptual Framework." *Policy Futures in Education,* 2003, *1*(2), 248–270.

Rowland, S. *The Enquiring University. Compliance and Contestation in Higher Education.* Maidenhead, Berkshire (England): The Society for Research into Higher Education (SRHE) and Open University Press, 2006.

Schoorinan, D. "The Pedagogical Implications of Diverse Conceptualizations of Internationalization: A U.S. Based Case Study." *Journal of Studies in International Education,* 1999, *3*(2), 19–46.

Slaughter, S. "National Higher Education Policies in a Global Economy." In J. Currie and J. Newson (eds.), *Universities and Globalization. Critical Perspectives,* 45–70. Thousand Oaks, Calif.: Sage Publications, 1998.

Stromquist, N. P. "Internationalization as a Response to Globalization: Radical Shifts in University Environments." *Higher Education,* 2007, *53*(1), 61–105.

Thune, T., and Welle-Strand, A. "ICT for and in Internationalization Processes. A Business School Case Study." *Higher Education,* 2005, *50*(4), 593–611.

Van der Wende, M. *Internationalising the Curriculum in Dutch Higher Education: An International Comparative Perspective.* The Hague: The Netherlands Organisation for International Cooperation in Higher Education (NUFFIC), 1996.

Van der Wende, M. "Internationalising the Curriculum in Dutch Higher Education: An International Comparative Perspective." *Journal of Studies in International Education,* 1997, *1*(2), 53–72.

Van der Wende, M. "The Central Role of Universities in a Global World: Final Report of the 52 CRE Bi-Annual Conference." In *European Universities, World Partners. CRE Action 115.* Geneva: CRE, Conference of European Rectors, 1999.

Van der Wende, M. "Internationalization Policies: About New Trends and Contrasting Paradigms." *Higher Education Policy,* 2001, *14*(3), 249–259.

Van Vught, F., Van der Wende, M., and Westerhejden, D. "Globalisation and Internationalisation: Policy Agendas Compared." In J. Enders and O. Fulton (eds.), *Higher Education in a Globalising World. International Trends and Mutual Observations. A Festschrift in Honour of Ulrich Teichler,* 103–121. Dordrecht, The Netherlands: Kluwer Academic Publishers, 2002.

CAROLIN KREBER *is a professor of higher education at the University of Edinburgh where she is also director of the Centre for Teaching, Learning and Assessment. She is also adjunct associate professor at the University of Alberta, Canada.*

2

*Market-driven in its efforts to increase revenue, interna-
tionalization at Niagara College Canada is in evidence
primarily at the institutional level and marginalized at
the academic level. However, a byproduct has been the
gradual evolution of internationalized academic programs and curricula as academic staff external to the
International Department become more sensitive to and
educated in the notion of internationalization.*

Reflections on Trends and Challenges in Internationalizing an Ontario Community College

Valerie L. Grabove

Niagara College Canada is a mid-sized college with 6,300 fulltime and 18,000 part-time students. For almost 20 years, the College's internationalization evolution has been the purview of the International Education and Development Division (IEED) and has included international projects, contracts, English-as-second language (ESL), international students in postsecondary programs, program development, foreign language study, and international exchanges. In Ontario, the Colleges of Applied Arts and Technology (CAATs) expect their International Departments to be funded by international student tuition and /or international projects (Galway, 2000).

This chapter describes how Niagara College has embraced internationalization using an entrepreneurial model. Two frameworks described in the literature capture the evolution of Niagara College's internationalization: academic capitalism and development of global competencies (Rhoades, 2005).

Introduction

Niagara College's mission is to provide education and training for a changing world by being enterprising, innovative, and globally connected. References to internationalization in College documents are contiguous with "entrepreneurial" and/or "value-added" language such as "innovative programs and services that have an entrepreneurial focus and contain value-added international

New Directions for Teaching and Learning, no. 118, Summer 2009   © Wiley Periodicals, Inc.
Published online in Wiley InterScience (www.interscience.wiley.com) • DOI: 10.1002/tl.349

components." References to "internationalization" and "globalization" are used interchangeably throughout College documents, but a clear definition of either term is lacking. In her study, Knight (1997) found that different stakeholders attach their own definition to internationalization and that, in the education sector, a barrier is the confusion regarding the meaning and importance of internationalization.

Although language in Niagara College's Strategic Plan situates internationalization within a market-driven, revenue-generating framework, a metric for student success suggests the nobler aspiration of internationalization as an educational process; for example, program reviews to evaluate value-added international components should ensure "international content and learning activities to provide domestic students with international awareness and international students with opportunities to contribute to and participate effectively in the learning process." Confusion regarding this metric is evident in program reviews described later in this chapter. Some faculty and staff understand internationalization as integrating international dimensions into their teaching as academic knowledge and/or respect for diversity of perspectives; however, the majority of faculty perceives internationalization as international projects, students, campus activities, and global opportunities.

Reduced funding has triggered competition for resources and students among higher education institutions. Since 1992, funding for Ontario Colleges has decreased by 17 percent whereas enrollments have increased by 16 percent (Colleges Ontario, 2007); in fact, government grants per student remain the lowest in Canada. Internationalization has become essential for revenue generation.

Market-driven to generate revenue, internationalization at Niagara College is a focus at the corporate level and marginalized at the academic level, although there is explicit agreement with Knight's definition of internationalization as "the process of integrating an international dimension into teaching/training, research, and service functions of a . . . college" (1997). Although programs have been created with an international academic focus, there is little evidence that an internationalization sensibility has been infused across college curricula except on an ad hoc basis by faculty whose experiences and philosophies of teaching include diversity and/or internationalization. However, the evolution of international programs and increased international activity has augmented awareness of internationalization. A recent example merits notice: during recent high school tours of the college, I overheard college student guides promoting volunteer opportunities at the college, namely, to be a "conversation partner" with an international student.

Ontario Colleges

Niagara College is one of several Ontario Colleges of Applied Arts and Technology (CAATs) created in 1965 and designed to be responsive to community needs and economic development. International activity was not included in the original mandate. In 2002, the Ontario Ministry of Training, Colleges and Universities (MTCU) revised the original mandate to include meeting global marketplace demands. In 2005, MTCU announced an additional $5 million to assist in the internationalization of Ontario's postsecondary education.

In Ontario, 24 CAATs serve a diverse population of learners including 5 percent who are international students. Not surprisingly, the majority of college-bound international students choose more multicultural urban areas; Niagara is considered a "rural college" with a noticeable lack of diversity.

Lack of diversity among our regional population and college faculty contributes a barrier, a lack of awareness, regarding internationalization. We regularly encounter lack of awareness that our ethnic or ESL students are not all international students (50 percent of our ESL population consists of new immigrants). The Niagara Region is considered slow in accepting diverse learners because of our demographics and limited worldview.

Internationalization Metrics. Despite the limited multicultural nature of our local community, Niagara College has been relatively successful in its recruitment efforts, and in terms of revenue generation, the figures are impressive. College international revenue ranks fourth—.8 percent of total operating revenue—after three Toronto CAATs with more than double the student population. For comparison, Niagara College's total operating budget ranks eleventh among Ontario CAATs.

International students make up 8 percent of our student population, a fairly large percentage considering our size and location. It is also significant that the 463 international students enrolled in sixty-one programs represent sixty-two countries. Although Niagara College's internationalization model is driven by economics (international students pay more than double the tuition fees of domestic students), recruitment of such a diverse population is indicative of our diversity values. A comparison of other colleges' international student statistics reveals that such a diverse international population is not the norm; at Niagara College, this diversity is not an accident. Castaneda (2004) suggests that such an increase in diversity benefits students from all backgrounds.

A 2007 report to the Board of Governors exemplified that we reached our goal to infuse each program with elements of internationalization; however, the examples suggest that the term "infuse each program" did not mean infusing internationalization into "curriculum." Of significance, however, is the increase in the number of programs with an international experience, which has increased over the life of the current strategic plan.

College internationalization metrics highlight international and ESL student enrollment and revenue, international projects, and numbers of staff and students involved. However, there is not a metric to measure integration of internationalization in the curriculum. Internationalization

NEW DIRECTIONS FOR TEACHING AND LEARNING • DOI: 10.1002/tl

examples in the Board Report include international student recruitment primarily in Business, Hospitality and Tourism, and Technology programs; the intercultural/international dimension afforded by social and academic interactions among students from over sixty countries; and numbers of faculty, staff, and students involved in international projects, placements, or internships.

In the same report, a listing of programs captured forty-seven as internationalized and eleven as engaged in overseas activities. It is questionable whether these examples mirror Knight's definition (1997) or the College metric described in the Strategic Plan: to ensure academic programs include "international content and learning activities to provide domestic students with international awareness and international students with opportunities to contribute to and participate effectively in the learning process." There is work to be done if internationalization of curriculum is to be realized. There is an assumption that the opportunity for social and academic interactions among international and domestic students and faculty is realized and provides international learning experiences. Vertesi (1999) cautions that these interactions should not be assumed.

MTCU oversees a review of standards, and each college's programs and delivery are to be consistent with these standards. Niagara College's program review identifies internationalization as one criterion, but a definition of internationalization is lacking. Seventeen programs recently reviewed reported meeting the internationalization criterion. Inspection of these reports demonstrates that the interpretation of internationalization is misunderstood or manipulated. Twelve programs identified international student enrollment as an example of meeting the criterion; one program described the cultural and experiential diversity offered by international students; two programs described international projects and partnerships; and only two programs presented international concepts, cross-cultural, and global issues in the curriculum. Ironically, one program reported that internationalization has not been incorporated; nevertheless, this same program includes courses such as sociology, public administration, ethics, diversity, and first nations. Clearly, the notion of internationalization is misunderstood (Bond, 2003).

Of the ninety-nine programs at Niagara College, nineteen feature courses dedicated to international, global or diversity education. Of these, eight are distinct international academic programs leading to global career opportunities, and each has faculty with international experiences: two Bachelor of Applied Business programs (International Commerce and Global Development and Hospitality Operations Management); Business Administration: International Business; International Business Management; Tourism Management—Business Development; and Teaching English as a Second Language. These specific programs are integral to the College's strategic plan; however, notions of a Global Competency framework (Rhoades, 2005) are evident within all nineteen programs by nature of the career paths they lead to such as Social Service Worker and Police Foundations.

Although there is an assumption that international students, projects, and exchanges create an internationalized college, and there is no question that these elements do influence the culture, faculty on the whole are not internationalized, an important foundation if we are to infuse internationalization throughout the curriculum. Khalideen (2006) cautions that most often, internationalization is restricted by the "limited knowledge of professors." The college cultivates international partnerships, which provide a limited number of faculty and students international experiences. One objective is that they will bring back other perspectives, which will translate into internationalized curricula; however, there isn't a metric to determine what is learned and how this learning is realized in the classroom. Although an increase in the college's international student population has raised awareness, the reality is that, unless the faculty recognizes the significance of targeted teaching and learning strategies, most often we see our international student populations unable to integrate or share learning with local students.

General Education and Internationalization at Niagara College

Evidently, if internationalization initiatives are to be successful and meaningful throughout the curriculum, the College and/or MTCU need to clearly define the standards. MTCU mandates that all Ontario college graduates take three to five General Education courses separate from their vocational fields of study, which foster consciousness of the diversity and complexity of society. General Education courses are categorized according to themes, two of which directly relate to our topic: Civic Life, and Social and Cultural Understanding. Civic Life courses should include curriculum related to diverse communities at local, national, and global levels, international issues, and Canada's place in the international community; Social and Cultural Understanding courses explore an understanding of the impact of cultural, social, ethnic, or linguistic characteristics.

A review of General Education courses at Niagara College suggests twenty-five courses that may include internationalized curricula, but further investigation would be required to confirm this. For example, courses such as Global Environmental Issues, World Religions, Understanding Society, French Language and Culture, Intercultural Communications, and others presumably integrate internationalization principles. Language courses open other possibilities as do Current Events, Exploring International Cuisine, and Workplace Culture. One would expect however that the effectiveness of internationalization relies on the experiences and knowledge of the faculty teaching the courses (Bond, Huang, and Qian, 2003).

My conversations with General Education faculty captured a number of courses enhanced with internationalism, global issues, and diversity including content and teaching and learning strategies. In particular, several recently hired faculty members have brought new ideas, experiences, and curricula.

NEW DIRECTIONS FOR TEACHING AND LEARNING • DOI: 10.1002/tl

As well, aggressive advocacy by the Chair, General Education, has increased awareness of the importance of General Education resulting in more electives being imbedded in vocational programs, which have heretofore resisted, citing lack of resources and full student timetables as rationales. A systemic approach to ensuring students have access to more General Education electives is being resourced and may result in more internationalized courses.

Furthermore, a review of all general education curricula to ensure compliance with MTCU and sound pedagogical principles has increased conversation among faculty and deans regarding effective curriculum development and where faculty development would enhance skills and knowledge. Although these discussions are not focused on internationalization, internationalization principles are part of the conversation.

Resourcing and Raising Awareness of Internationalization

The International Education and Development Division (IEDD) has been instrumental in raising the profile and importance of internationalization, but IEDD is mostly separated from the post-secondary world of the College. However, their new strategic plan (2007–2012) addresses this separation with goals to integrate, foster international competencies among faculty, and actively participate in professional development activities. If appropriately resourced and realized, these goals could be transformative.

As well as the internationalization initiatives described earlier, a number of other College initiatives support international and/or intercultural understanding and skills, and are worth reviewing.

International Department. The strategic placement of the International Department beside the cafeteria and a central, high profile gathering space on campus has increased IEDD profile and that of our international population. Although this would likely not be highlighted in a multicultural urban college, it is significant in our more homogeneous rural community. An international club includes many domestic students, and Global Connections, a volunteer program, which partners international students with domestic students, has met with great success—over 300 students participate.

Special opportunities that are frequently publicized emerge for students and faculty such as a recent culinary excursion to Portugal; students cooked at the Canadian Embassy with a professor/chef, showcased Canadian foods and wines, and signed a partnership agreement with a Portuguese college.

Between 1999–2006, the college provided one-hundred twenty-four students with international experiences and plans to expand international opportunities for interns, co-op placements, and graduates. According to the Manager of International Services and Recruitment, the College never submits an international project proposal unless it offers opportunities for students.

Faculty/Staff Development. A new faculty development initiative, curriculum coaching, includes three seconded professors in a peer coaching team; it's no accident that each has a transformative, reflective, learner-centered approach to teaching, including international experience. In fact, one professor was seconded from the International Department, a move that will help blur the lines of separation between the international and postsecondary divisions. As the team designs the new curriculum coaching program, their discussions include notions of raising faculty awareness of the importance of diversity, globalization, and internationalization within the curriculum.

All newly hired faculty attend a three-year faculty development program, which offers teaching and learning workshops and discussions on topics relevant to today's college environment. Opportunities to develop teaching skills related to internationalism, interculturalism, and related topics are included alongside discussions reflecting on philosophies of practice.

As well as international projects, faculty are supported during sabbaticals and pre-paid leaves to make international connections for their own learning. They have recurring opportunities to share international experiences during our annual Professional Development (PD) Leaves Showcase series and a lunch series, Internationally Speaking, designed to "increase IQ" (International Quotient).

Occasionally, professional and organizational development activities are designed to raise awareness of diversity, multiculturalism, and internationalism. One special college conference, "Understanding Our Students," attracted more than three-hundred fifty faculty and staff to learn about, discuss, and reflect on issues related to this topic. A controversial and compelling keynote speaker, concurrent workshops, student panels, and roundtable discussions throughout the day made an impact with some lasting effect.

Courses and Programs. This year, more language courses, Mandarin, Japanese, and Spanish, have been introduced as electives. As well, some General Arts and Science courses are being redesigned to engage students in learning about internationalism, multiculturalism, and diversity.

In 2006, Citizenship and Immigration Canada funded three new College programs to help newcomers to Canada find employment and build skills: "Advanced Language for Employment" for foreign-trained professionals, a Pre-Apprentice Cook Training program, and English for Academic Preparation.

To eliminate systemic barriers of access, Niagara College, in partnership with Heritage Canada, is developing outreach pilots to encourage youth from diverse populations to attend college.

On-Campus Student Activities and Employment. A number of on-campus activities and special events, volunteer opportunities, and student clubs support internationalization. A philosophy club engages faculty and students in weekly discussions, including topics related to multiculturalism and diversity. A special funding project subsidizes college departments that hire international students to allow them to learn from workplace experience; international students work in the college greenhouse, labs, winery, dining room, and offices, as well as with environmental reclamation projects and co-op assignments.

Conclusion and Recommendations

A key question needs to be raised: How does internationalization of the college translate as evidence of learning in a competency-based curriculum? Though great strides have been made to raise the internationalization quotient of Niagara College, metrics for internationalization need clarification, and the integration of international, intercultural, and global dimensions should be imbedded in all programs, projects, and services as one of the competencies to be measured in our external and internal audits.

Niagara College's programs must meet MTCU standards and offer education relevant to employers' and students' needs, including key vocational skills and broader skills and knowledge. Mechanisms are in place to review quality, relevancy, and currency of programs. In our globalized environment, internationalization, with a clear definition, should be one of the mandated criteria for all programs.

Currently, unless (1) programs are integrated with the College Strategic Plan and academic priorities, business plans, and international initiatives; (2) international students are enrolled; or (3) professors are knowledgeable, skilled, and believe in internationalization, it is conceivable that some students will graduate without any international/intercultural learning. Although the literature suggests that faculty will report discipline incongruity as their rationale for not including internationalization (Bond, Huang, and Qian, 2003), Ontario's higher education system emphasizes that, to be successful in a globalized society, our students require international competencies.

The literature reports that faculty lack international knowledge, experience, and/or the skills necessary to foster internationalization, which suggests the need for concentrated resources for professional development. The college goal to infuse internationalization into every program is a noble one, but to be successful college-wide, a systemic strategy, including professional development, committed resources, and committed leadership, is necessary to achieve this goal.

Niagara College needs to be explicit in its definition of internationalization, and related values need to be infused throughout the curriculum and throughout college practices. In a competency- and outcomes-based educational system, internationalization should to be imbedded within the curriculum of all programs and designed as a measurable outcome of student learning. A key initiative that should have a major impact in integrating internationalization throughout the college is the new strategic plan and vision of our International Department: to become fully integrated with the college.

References

Bond, S., Huang, J., and Qian, J. *The Role of Faculty in Internationalizing the Undergraduate Curriculum and Classroom Experience.* Ottawa: Canadian Bureau of International Education, 2003.

Castaneda, C. R. *Teaching and Learning in Diverse Classrooms.* New York: Routledge Faimler, 2004.

Colleges Ontario. "2007 Environmental Scan: An Analysis of Trends and Issues Affecting Ontario, 2007." Retrieved Feb. 14, 2008, from http://www.collegesontario.org.

Galway, A. *Going Global: Ontario Colleges of Applied Arts and Technology, International Student Recruitment and the Export of Education.* Toronto: Ontario Institute for Studies in Higher Education, University of Toronto, 2000.

Khalideen, R. "Internationalizing the Curriculum in Canadian Universities: Considering the Influences of Power, Politics and Ethics." Paper presented at York University, Toronto: Internationalizing Canada's Universities: Practices, Challenges, and Opportunities, March 2006.

Knight, J. "A Shared Vision? Stakeholders' Perspectives on the Internationalization of Higher Education in Canada." *Journal of Studies in International Education,* 1997, *1*(1), 27–44. Retrieved March 23, 2007, from http://www.jsi.sagepub.com

Rhoades, G. "Capitalism, Academic Style, and Shared Governance." Academe, 2005, 91(3). Retrieved February 2, 2008, from http://www.aaup.org/AAUP/pubsres/academe/2005/MJ/Feat/rhod.htm.

Vertesi, C. "Students as Agents of Change." In S. Bond and L. Lemasson (eds.), *A New World of Knowledge: Canadian Universities and Globalization.* Ottawa: International Development Research Centre, 1999.

VALERIE L. GRABOVE is chair of the Centre for Educational and Professional Development at Niagara College Canada and an Award of Excellence recipient for her work in organizational, faculty, and staff development.

3

An internationalized curriculum requires that we extend our actions far beyond concerns of course content to include pedagogies that promote cross-cultural understanding and facilitate the development of the knowledge, skills, and values that will enable students, both domestic and international, to successfully engage with others in an increasingly interconnected and interdependent world.

Education for World-Mindedness: Beyond Superficial Notions of Internationalization

Geraldine Van Gyn, Sabine Schuerholz-Lehr, Catherine Caws, Allison Preece

Internationalisation of curriculum . . . cannot be done by a university edict but through the creative utilisation of the imagination of all those who make up that university. This imagination itself needs to be globalised in ways that are both self reflexive and critical.

Rizvi, 2000, p. 193

Introduction

As part of our university-wide effort on internationalization, a committee of university educators (both faculty and staff) was asked to lead an initiative to internationalize curricula. The majority of the committee was either formally linked with the university's learning and teaching center or had been closely involved with the center and its work on curriculum design reform. Our initial activities included a broad review of current internationalization efforts in courses and programs at the University of Victoria in British Columbia and elsewhere. This review revealed a number of instances in which international content and examples were included in courses. Specific introductory course activities to acknowledge the diverse backgrounds of students, and genuine, and more pervasive, actions related to inclusive,

NEW DIRECTIONS FOR TEACHING AND LEARNING, no. 118, Summer 2009 © Wiley Periodicals, Inc.
Published online in Wiley InterScience (www.interscience.wiley.com) • DOI: 10.1002/tl.350

nondiscriminatory language were also identified. Although these initiatives are laudable, most are not widespread and reflect a surface or technical approach to internationalization of curricula. What we mean by this is that the main impetus for internationalization typically comes from university policy, the dominant Western paradigm for teaching and learning remains intact, and, consequently, internationalization efforts frequently do not go beyond additions, which are not well integrated with the rest of the curriculum. Given our own work on curriculum design, and informed by the literature review, we realized that the type of curriculum change that we envisioned would be multifaceted and difficult, perhaps even extending beyond the bounds of our own understanding of internationalization of curriculum. For higher education curricula to be inclusive of international students and prepare all students with intercultural knowledge and competence, a fundamental change in perspective on teaching and learning on the part of those responsible for curriculum development, and equally important, an expanded view of internationalization is required.

Although the term "internationalization" and, consequently, the phrase "internationalization of the curriculum" is still highly contested (Green and Olson, 2003; Schoorman, 2000), it appears to be the most commonly used term in the literature. Therefore, we will use the term internationalization to describe the focus of the educational development work that we have done, but we think that "education for world-mindedness"[1] best describes what we hope university and college educators can deliver as a result of this initiative and is what all our students will experience.

In the following sections, we will explain our understanding of internationalization of the curriculum and some implications for higher education and discuss how we identified a particular educational development approach that we believe is very effective in the advancement of an internationalized curriculum and discuss its theoretical foundations. We will then describe the educational development intervention that we employ to engage university educators in the process of internationalizing the curriculum. Finally, we will review some of the results of the research that we conducted on our educational development intervention and our plans for further refinements of the intervention.

Our Perspective on Internationalization of the Curriculum in Higher Education

Internationalization of the curriculum is a complex concept that reflects the intricate relationship between historical context, political orientations, dominant epistemologies, and perceptions on the use of knowledge, as well as conceptions of teaching and learning. An internationalized curriculum will reflect the plurality of knowledge, and will also engage students in critical inquiry of the diverse sources and contexts of knowledge, and the factors that have shaped such knowledge. An internationalized curriculum requires that we extend our actions far beyond concerns of course content to include pedagogies that promote cross-cultural understanding and facilitate the development of the knowledge, skills, and values that will enable students, both domestic and international, to successfully engage with others in an increasingly interconnected and interdependent world. As such, it demands a different paradigm for teaching and learning than the positivistic model of education that currently dominates in Western colleges and universities. One of the most significant challenges to internationalization of the curriculum arises from entrenched perspectives and long held beliefs (Bennett, 1993), not only on internationalization, but also on the process of curriculum design, which includes perspectives on teaching and learning.

There has been considerable growth in awareness of the inadequacy of conventional approaches to teaching and learning to meet the academic needs of a diverse student population, which includes a growing number of international students. Nonetheless, there has not been a substantive change in the way in which curriculum in higher education is designed and implemented. This lack of progress is predictable, as it is college and university educators who hold the majority of the power with regards to the curriculum across programs, and particularly within their own courses. As subject-matter specialists, their main concern, expertise, and interest is in the content of their courses, and one should expect that content will be the target for change, in efforts to internationalize the curriculum. Generally, these changes take the form of international example of concepts and principles. In addition, and usually with the influence of the larger university community on social practices within the institution, one would also expect to see other types of additions to course material and practices such as the use of culturally inclusive language and information for international students about language support. These types of changes reflect an early and relatively underdeveloped view of what constitutes internationalization of curriculum. The process of adding on international elements to a course is consistent with the view of many university and college educators on the curriculum design process. Our observations are not intended to suggest that university and college educators are resistant to the notion of internationalization, but there appear to be limitations on two levels. First, the concept of internationalization and its contribution to higher education is inadequately understood by most (Green and Olson, 2003). Vaira (2004) reflects that ". . . the relationships between [internationalization] and higher education seem to be acuter, perplexing and open to multiple and divergent accounts" (p. 484). Getting to the heart of what internationalization means in higher education is not a simple matter. On a second level, most postsecondary educators simply do not have the pedagogical knowledge or skills to make the sophisticated changes that reflect a comprehensive implementation of the concept and therefore, with all good intentions, address internationalization with course changes that are at a fairly superficial or technical level. The technical level response to internationalizing the curriculum is reflective of the shortcomings with the preparation of graduate students for the teaching role in higher education. Saroyan and Amundsen (2004) suggest that without adequate pedagogical preparation, university and college educators rely on models of curriculum design that they have experienced and observed during their undergraduate and graduate programs. As a result, many university and college educators, with little else to draw on, will perpetuate traditional approaches and perspectives of teaching, learning, and course planning that we know to be relatively ineffective given the current student population (Biggs, 2003).

To proceed on internationalization of the curriculum, university and college educators must understand internationalization in a very profound way and then be able to translate this understanding into curricular changes. Considering the type and extent of the complex changes to curriculum required by internationalization, we suggest that postsecondary educators need a much greater degree of support than is currently available in most institutions to advance this very complex process. Top-down models of curriculum internationalization, sometimes led by a team of consultants, appear to be ineffective in creating the necessary understanding and commitment from university and college educators for this process.

Finding the Right Educational Development Vehicle

As a result of our initial research and deliberations, we determined that the process of internationalizing the curriculum, if it was to be done in a meaningful way, begins with capturing the "hearts and minds" of university and college educators with regards to internationalization and its implications for curriculum in higher education. A substantial learning experience should follow to enable the development of pedagogical knowledge and skills to design such a curriculum along with support for implementation of their proposed changes to their courses and programs.

For several years prior to the internationalization initiative, we had successfully conducted the Course Design Workshop (CDW) for over 100 university and college educators. The CDW was developed by members of the Centre for University Teaching and Learning, McGill University in Montreal, Canada (Saroyan and Amundsen, 2004). This five-day intensive workshop is informed by two theoretical perspectives: transformative learning (Mezirow, 1991) and teacher growth (Ramsden, 2003). The particular orientation to teaching and learning that underpins the CDW is learning-centered and collaborative in nature. For a detailed description of the CDW and the research on its impact, please refer to Saroyan and Amundsen (2004).

We observed several general changes in our participants in the CDW: significant growth in the understanding of the need for a learning-centered curriculum and the curriculum design implications for such an orientation; the development of participants' capacity to design and implement learning outcomes, instructional strategies, and assessment methods that are congruent with the learning-centered orientation; and a renewed or new-found sense of enthusiasm and confidence about teaching. These outcomes are similar to those reported by Saroyan and Amundsen (2004) from their research of the CDW over a period of ten years.

We agreed that the CDW processes would provide the opportunity for participants to engage intensively with the concept of internationalization and with effective teaching and learning concepts. We also concluded that we could make changes to the materials and format that would place an internationalization lens on the workshop activities. In choosing this particular educational intervention, we also committed to a comprehensive and systematic approach that engages a relatively small number of faculty and instructional staff for an extensive period as opposed to implementing a less-intensive intervention, which potentially would engage more people. We reasoned that the complex nature of internationalization of curriculum warranted the intensive engagement of participants that could be achieved through the CDW.

Capturing Hearts and Minds: Transformative Learning

As we previously suggested, the first goal in an educational development activity to promote internationalization of the curriculum must be to engage university and college educators in a critical examination of their assumptions about this concept, as well as those about teaching and learning. These concepts, particularly the latter, most likely have been uncritically assimilated from their student experiences. Any substantial change to one's actions, such as those we are seeking in internationalizing the curriculum, is usually preceded by a transformation in perspective. Mezirow (1991) refers to this as "the process of becoming critically aware of how and why our assumptions have come to constrain the way we perceive, understand, and feel about our world; changing these structures of habitual expectation to make possible a more inclusive, discriminating, and integrating perspective; and, finally, making choices or otherwise acting upon these new understandings" (p. 167). He suggests that this occurs in the following phases:

- Acknowledgement of a disorienting dilemma
- Self-examination and critical assessment of beliefs and assumptions
- Recognition that comparable changes in perspective have been experienced by others
- Consideration and investigation of new orientations or actions
- Development of an action plan
- Acquiring knowledge and skills for implementing the plan
- Testing and sharing of the plan

- Development of confidence and enthusiasm in the new perspective and actions
- Reintegration into life on the basis of new perspectives

For these phases to occur within the CDW, adequate time for critical reflection, opportunities for collaboration with peers, and sufficient resources (e.g., reference materials and knowledgeable facilitators) are necessary conditions. The transformation of perspective is completed through the testing of the new perspective in known situations. The transformative learning process explicated by Mezirow's theory is predominately "rational, analytical, and cognitive" (Grabove, 1997, p. 90), which we have found has an attraction for many academics. There has been substantial criticism of the emphasis placed on the rational process of critical reflection as the key to perspective transformation (Taylor, 1998). As an alternative theoretical explanation, the work of Boyd and Myers (1988) has been applied to explain the process of transformative learning as imaginative, creative, and intuitive, with an emphasis on affective rather than rational ways of thinking (Cranton, 1994). Nonetheless, Grabove (1997) maintains that the essential elements of "humanism, emancipation, autonomy, critical reflection, equity, self-knowledge, participation, communication and discourse" (p. 90) are common to both views. We concluded that the transformative learning processes in the CDW, which are systematic and logical but also allow for creative and intuitive ways of thinking, would engage both the "hearts and minds" of our academic participants.

Growth in Learning-Centered Teaching

The other theoretical foundation of the CDW is teacher growth, particularly in the manner envisioned by Ramsden (2003) in which learning-centered teaching and a learning-centered curriculum is the outcome. This theoretical perspective focuses on the active and meaningful engagement of the learner with the course content and processes. What students do and the degree to which they do it is the most important concern of the educator. Related to this educational orientation are the notions of self-regulation, metacognition, and critical thinking. For a comprehensive discussion of learning-centered approaches to curriculum, please refer to Biggs (2003), Ramsden (2003), or Fink (2003).

There is an increasing understanding among members of the higher education community that this orientation to teaching and learning is far more effective than the conventional transmission orientations, which have dominated practices in our institutions. Not only is the effectiveness of a learning-centered curriculum supported by extensive cognitive, social, and neural psychological research (e.g., Bransford, Brown, and Cocking, 2000), but as Biggs (2003) notes it is the most appropriate approach for the inclusion of students with diverse cultural and educational backgrounds. Focusing on what students are doing and using active and engaging methods is the basis of good teaching—and good teaching reaches all students.

In our experience with the CDW, we had observed that when participants were introduced and engaged with active and learning-focused teaching methods and when they came to understand the significance of the research on the efficacy of these methods, there was a clear and immediate shift in perspective on how they should be teaching. As the CDW experience continues, participants embrace the idea of an aligned curriculum where all "pieces" (content, learning outcomes, instructional strategies, assessment methods) are related to the others. Not only does it appeal to their logic, but it provides them with a systematic process and tools upon which they can plan their courses. Having both the tools and the knowledge to explain why the curriculum development process and its learning orientation are critical to student success is a powerful combination, and we observe radical changes in both the views and actions of participants.

Given our observations of the changes in our CDW participants, their subsequent curriculum activities, and the current literature, particularly the views of Biggs (2003), we concluded that many of the CDW curriculum processes would be compelling for university and college educators in their efforts to internationalize the curriculum.

The Course Redesign Workshop for Internationalization

Critical Elements. As we were adding the layer of internationalization to the CDW, yet retaining the same time commitment and organizational format, we had to ensure that the crucial elements of the workshop to which the process of transformative learning had been attributed (see Saroyan and Amundsen, 2004) were retained.

Consequently, the following features were prominent in the Course Redesign for Internationalization Workshop (CRIW):

- Current and engaging reading materials on learning-centered curriculum design to prepare the participant for each section of the workshop
- Task-specific collegial interaction interwoven with individual activities and in-depth interactions with facilitators
- Adequate time and sufficient structure for critical reflection on current assumptions and practice and for plans to revise current practice
- Sufficient document of participants' contributions (videotaping of presentations and production of materials, e.g., concept maps, written learning outcomes) to provide participants the opportunity to reflect on the changes they were proposing
- Opportunities for collegial critique, particularly across disciplinary areas
- Inclusion of the four fundamental phases of aligned curriculum design (content, learning outcomes, instructional strategies, assessment methods)

Like the CDW, the CRIW engages participants in 30 hours of interactive work with their peers and the facilitators over a five-day period. In addition, readings to inform their work and the preparation of materials reflecting the redesign of their courses that they will present to their peers on the following day require that the participants spend approximately two hours in their evenings at these tasks during the workshop period. Many of our participants report that the weeklong experience requires a singular focus on the workshop activities and that the intensity of the experience helps to maintain their enthusiasm and engagement in the process. The length of time and intensity of work required by the CDW and CRIW is, we believe, another critical element.

Preparation for the CRIW. Participants are recruited for the CRIW through department and faculty administrators and through the usual channels for communication used by the learning and teaching center for their educational development activities. All participants complete a comprehensive questionnaire prior to the CRIW that helps to reveal their current perspective on internationalization, educational practices, intentions for the workshop, and other details that will help the facilitators to anticipate participants' needs. From their responses, we find that participants, in general, are (1) experiencing a disorienting dilemma (Mezirow, 1991) in their courses, in that their current practices are not as successful as they once were; or (2) they have a clear commitment to internationalization and want to do better, but do not know how; or (3) both. Overall, responses on the pre-CRIW questionnaire indicate that participants' views on internationalization are underdeveloped and their concerns are centered on the rise in numbers of international students in their classes and the challenges presented by these students (e.g., language issues, resistance to group and active learning, and issues related to academic integrity).

Prior to the workshop, participants receive a binder that contains a detailed timetable of activities, handouts that will be used in the workshop, and readings that are applicable to each session in the CRIW. Participants are requested to complete several readings prior to the beginning of the workshop. Other readings are identified for each of the days of the course, and participants are encouraged to use these to inform their work.

Format and Activities. As previously stated, the CRIW, like the CDW is organized around four major activities: explication and representation of the content through a concept map, development of course-level learning outcomes, identification of the general approach to instructional strategies, and development of a general plan for assessment. The deliverables associated with the workshop are a general curriculum plan for their course and a completed course outline. In addition, the CRIW includes the initial activities of in-depth discussion of internationalization and implications for curriculum development and the creation of a concept map, representing each participant's view of internationalization. This map is used throughout the workshop to inform curricular decision and is open to modification as participants' understanding of the concept deepens. Table 3.1 contains the timetable, a brief description of activities for each day of the CRIW, and the related outcomes suggested for each activity.

Throughout the workshop, facilitators model active learning and collegial collaboration. As Saroyan and Amundsen (2004) found in their research, there is significant value to working in small multidisciplinary groups. Participants often find common ground on many issues, which improves the cross-disciplinary dialogue. Input from colleagues in other disciplines provides different perspectives and insights and expands participants' repertoire of curriculum design responses as well.

The weeklong experience is intense and effortful for participants, and therefore, we use a number of facilitators (four to six, depending on the number of participants, in a ratio of 1:4) to provide support and feedback.

Research on the CRIW. Consistent with our commitment to the scholarship of teaching and learning, we conducted research on the first implementation of the CRIW to insure that we were fulfilling the learning outcomes for the workshop and to inform changes to subsequent workshops (Schuerholz-Lehr, Caws, Van Gyn, and Preece, 2007). In general, the qualitative analysis of participants' feedback and the artifacts that they produced clearly indicated that they were undergoing a significant shift in their perspective on internationalization and curriculum design. This perspective transformation continued after the CRIW, as evidenced by interviews conducted three months later. Likely, this is indicative of the complexity of internationalization and the challenge of translating their growing understanding into elements of their curriculum design. Two other major themes that we identified from the analysis were an increased willingness to engage in curriculum change, and an awareness of the contradictions that were evident in their past practice and in institutional practices, in general. We felt that this was of considerable importance, as we agree with Trahar's (2007) comment that "It is [very rare] to find practitioner researchers reflecting critically on the impact of diversity on their practice and indeed on themselves" (p. 9).

In general, the format of the CRIW and the embedded activities appeared to promote the perspective transformation on internationalization for which we had hoped. Participants moved along "a developmental continuum of engagement from technical observance towards much more relational participation" (Rizvi, 2000). In addition, we noted a change in perspective on university teaching similar to that experienced in the CDW. Participants' understanding of an aligned curriculum were reflected in their initial attempts in developing clear and comprehensive learning outcomes, active and engaging learning activities as part of their instructional plan, and inclusive assessment methods that promote learning. Participants commented that the opportunity to apply their new curriculum design skills to

Table 3.1. Timeline and Activities for the Course Redesign for Internationalization Workshop (CRIW)

Day	Time period	Activity	Outcome
1	8:30 a.m. to 12 p.m.	Introductions. Review of workshop topics and process. Review of participants' responses to pre-CRIW survey. Group discussion of Int. Ind CM of Int. (F)	Develop a community. Feel comfortable with CRIW operations. Articulate coherent position on Int in higher education. Develop CM of Int to guide future work.
1	1:00 to 4:30 p.m.	Review and peer presentations of CM of Int. CM exercise applied to course under review. (F) Videotaped presentation* of preliminary course CM. Feedback questionnaire.*	Develop CM of course content to guide future work. Increase capacity to give and receive feedback (peer and cross-disciplinary) and to self-assess.* Express progress and needs.*
2	8:30 a.m. to 12 p.m.	Review of feedback.* Review and discussion of the concept of Int. Inter session on developing LOs and discussion of LOs specific to Int. Ind work on LOs specific to Int of course. (F)	Articulate and demonstrate need for alignment between course content and LOs.
2	1:00 to 4:30 p.m.	Continued Ind work on Int LOs. (F)	Develop clearer LOs (general and Int).
3	8:30 a.m. to 12 p.m.	Inter session on instructional strategies (IS) congruent with Int. GW on examples of Int IS. (F)	Expand on concept of Int. Increase capability to use aligned model of CD. Improve design of IS to promote deep learning.

3	1:00 to 4:30 p.m.	Ind. work on IS plan for own course. (F)	Develop general IS plan and several specific examples related to LOs.
4	8:30 a.m. to 12 p.m.	Inter session on A&E of LOs and the development of descriptive criteria (rubrics). GW on A techniques congruent with discussions on Int. (F)	Increase capability to use aligned model of CD, particularly relationship of A techniques to LOs. Design assessment both for learning and evaluation purposes.
4	1:00 to 4:30 p.m.	Indiv. work on A&E plan linked back to LOs and general rubrics.	Develop general A plan and one specific example.
5	8:30 a.m. to 12 p.m.	Inter discussion on views on Int of curriculum and need for support and experiences for students. Inter session on progress of Int of the curriculum initiative (scholarship of teaching and learning). Ind work on outlines of redesigned course. (F)	Refine Int CM. Increase capability to articulate own position on Int of the curriculum. Produce Int course outline.
5	1:00 to 2:30 p.m.	Poster session of course outlines. Celebration of completion of CRIW.	Experience sense of belonging to community of scholarly teachers. Feel enthusiastic for teaching and concept of Int.
Follow-up Phase		Follow-up questionnaire to assess success of CRIW. Invitation to join CRIW peers in informal meetings to share successes.	Further refine CRIW processes. Develop community of scholars interested in Int of curriculum.

Note. A = assessment; A&E = assessment and evaluation; CD = curriculum design; CM = concept map (mapping); F = facilitator support; GW = group work; Ind = individual; Int = internationalization; Inter = interactive; IS = instructional strategies; LOs = learning outcomes.

*Any item marked with an asterisk occurs every day and thus we do not repeat it in our table nor do we repeat their associated LOs.

a course that they were currently teaching was of great value, but they felt that more practice was needed before they felt fully confident about these processes. Most gratifying were comments that reflected Biggs' (2003) views that, fundamentally, the most important contribution instructors could make to the internationalization of the curriculum was good teaching. For a more in-depth description of the research methods and findings, please refer to Schuerholz-Lehr et al. (2007).

Future Plans

The demand for both the CRIW and the CRW has grown with each imple-mentation, suggesting that participants are sharing their positive experi-ences with their colleagues. In a review of the CRIW, those who had acted as facilitators commented on the time pressure to enable participants to explore fully internationalization and its various manifestations in curricu-lum and to give them sufficient time to develop an understanding and to practice the curriculum design skills that are the foundation of the work-shop. Given that critical reflection and collegial interaction are the processes central to perspective transformation, we are exploring alternative delivery schemes that may relieve some of the time pressure in the CRIW.

Conclusion

The commitment of our university educators to participate in the CRIW and the support of the institution for the workshop is unusual in a society that moves at a rapid pace and is used to learning through "sound bites." Spending time in critical reflection demands that we slow down and spend a sufficient amount of time to reveal and challenge the ways in which we think and act. It is only through the commitment of time and effort that the CRIW participants are able to arrive at a level of understanding that they can make the following observations:

> (I) hope to construct a learning experience where students go beyond learn-ing about various phenomena and learn how they might manifest differently depending on the method of inquiry or geographical or psychological place from which they emanate. (Participant from Sociology, CRIW No. 1)

> I no longer think of a place on the globe when I hear 'international' or 'inter-nationalization'—I now think of a place with the mind's eye. (Participant from Education, CRIW No. 1)

We believe that the progress made by each educator who completes the CRIW has an effect on curriculum that goes beyond their individual courses. The participants report that they feel empowered to act on internationalizing the curriculum as they have a vocabulary, a set of skills, and a deepened understanding of the issues with which they can influence others.

References

Bennett, M. J. "Towards Ethnorelativism: A Developmental Model of Intercultural Sensitivity." In R. M. Paige (ed.), *Education for the Intercultural Experience.* Yarmouth, ME: Intercultural Press, 1993.

Biggs, J. *Teaching for Quality Learning in Higher Education.* (2nd ed.) Maidenhead, Berkshire: Open University Press, 2003.

Boyd, R. D., and Myers, J. G. "Transformative Education." *International Journal of Lifelong Education,* 7(4), 261–284, 1988.

Bransford, J., Brown, A., and Cocking, R. (eds.). *How People Learn: Brain, Mind, Experience, and School.* Washington, DC: National Academies Press, 2000.

Cranton, P. *Understanding and Promoting Transformation: A Guide for Educators of Adults.* San Francisco: Jossey-Bass, 1994.

Fink, D. *Creating Significant Learning Experiences: An Integrated Approach to Designing College Courses.* San Francisco: Jossey-Bass, 2003.

Grabove, V. "The Many Facets of Transformative Learning Theory and Practice." In P. Cranton (ed.), *Transformative Learning in Action: Insights from Practice.* New Directions for Adult and Continuing Education, no. 74. San Francisco: Jossey-Bass, 1997.

Green, M., and Olson, C. *Internationalizing the Campus: A User's Guide.* Washington, DC: American Council on Education, 2003.

Mezirow, J. *Transformative Dimensions of Adult Learning.* San Francisco: Jossey-Bass, 1991.

Ramsden, P. *Learning to Teach in Higher Education.* (2nd ed.) London: Routledge Falmer, 2003.

Rizvi, F. "Internationalisation of Curriculum, 2000." Retrieved June 3, 2007, from http://www.pvci.rmit.edu.au/ioc/back/icpfr.pdf.

Saroyan, A., and Amundsen, C. (eds.) *Rethinking Teaching in Higher Education.* Sterling, VA: Stylus Publishing, 2004.

Schoorman, D. "What Really Do We Mean By 'Internationalization'?" *Contemporary Education,* 71(4), 5–11, 2000.

Schuerholz-Lehr, S., Caws, C., Van Gyn, G., and Preece, A. "Internationalizing the Higher Education Curriculum: An Emerging Model for Transforming Faculty Perspectives." *Canadian Journal of Higher Education,* 37(1), 67–94, 2007.

Taylor, E. W. "The Theory and Practice of Transformative Learning: A Critical Review." *Information Series no. 374.* Columbus: ERIC Clearinghouse on Adult, Career, and Vocational Education, Center on Education and Training for Employment, College of Education, the Ohio State University, 1998.

Trahar, S. *Teaching and Learning: The International Higher Education Landscape.* Clifton, Bristol: Higher Education Academy Subject Centre for Education ESCalate, 2007.

Vaira, M. "Globalization and Higher Education Organization Change: A Framework for Analysis?" *Higher Education,* 48(4), 483–510, 2004.

Note

1. "Worldmindedness" was a term that was hotly debated, along with others, in the second implementation of the CRIW. It was this term that participants agreed upon and which we continue to use. We thank those University of Victoria faculty and staff CRIW participants for this contribution to our work.

GERALDINE VAN GYN, is a professor in the Faculty of Education (Kinesiology) and past director of the University of Victoria Learning and Teaching Centre. Her research focuses on learning conditions that foster cognitive engagement and support critical thinking.

SABINE SCHUERHOLZ-LEHR is the assistant director of International Affairs at the University of Victoria and is currently completing a PhD in Educational Studies with a focus on internationalization in higher education.

CATHERINE CAWS is an assistant professor in the Humanities Faculty, department of French at the University of Victoria. Her areas of research include language teaching, computer-assisted language learning, and the development of multiple literacies in higher education.

ALLISON PREECE is an associate professor of Language, Literacy, and Early Childhood in the Faculty of Education at the University of Victoria. For the past decade, she has worked with teachers and teacher educators in Macedonia, Armenia, Pakistan, and Kyrgyzstan on issues of critical engagement.

Internationalizing higher education is not simply a matter of adding international content. If one of the roles of higher education is to prepare students to survive and thrive in an uncertain, globalized world, we and our students have to develop a multicultural attitude that is both sensitive to, and appreciative of, cultural diversity.

From the Inside Out: Learning to Understand and Appreciate Multiple Voices Through Telling Identities

Bobbie Turniansky, Smadar Tuval, Ruth Mansur, Judith Barak, Ariela Gidron

The increasingly important international dimension in education calls for awareness of the world's complexity and interdependence, communication skills across cultures, and appreciation of cultural differences as resources (Hobbs and Chernotsky, 2007). According to Gallini and Zhang (1997), an internationalized curriculum is one that values and includes multicultural perspectives. It is an inclusive curriculum that promotes multidirectional flows of ideas and values through valuing the culture, background, and experience of all students. We would like to argue that internationalizing higher education is not simply a matter of adding international content. Understanding comes through interaction, through listening to your own voice and that of others. If one of the roles of higher education is to prepare students to survive and thrive in an uncertain, globalized world, our students and we have to develop a multicultural attitude that is both sensitive to, and appreciative of, cultural diversity.

Widening our horizons to include the other in our realm of understanding is crucial for everyday interactions and is even greater in professional contexts. In practice, the problem with such a multicultural attitude is embedded in our limited ability as individual human beings to grasp the

other in terms different than our own, and as "cultural beings" to extend our cultural horizons of understanding beyond the boundaries shaped by our own contextually situated life stories. Understanding the other person's culture demands an extra effort on the part of the knower, which is not without risk. As Delpit (1988) reminds us, "We do not really see through our eyes or hear through our ears, but through our beliefs. To put our beliefs on hold is to cease to exist as ourselves for a moment—and that is not easy" (p. 297).

When we talk about internationalization in higher education, we can talk about content (what we teach) or process (how we teach). However, we would prefer to talk about what is learned and how it is learned. From a constructivist point of view, learning is constructed by the learners through collaboration with others within a cultural context, not something passed on to them by a teacher.

In this chapter, we discuss a workshop we developed in light of our understanding that personal and professional identity develops within social–cultural contexts and is influenced by those contexts (Lurie, 2000). This workshop, "Cultural Identity—Personal and Professional," was created to help our students understand their own cultural identities and its influence on their professional practice.

In what follows, we first introduce the context in which the workshop takes place. Then we present the assumptions behind the workshop and describe how it works. In the next sections, we discuss the conditions necessary for a workshop like this to succeed, as well as problems and dilemmas that merit further consideration. We end with a brief look at some of the ethical questions this type of work raises.

Although we are focusing on a workshop that is part of a teacher education program, we contend that the same principles hold true for any profession. In many professions, the central questions are questions of judgment about what is "correct" or appropriate in different life situations and therefore, the issue of cultural and professional identity should be placed in the center of any professional development process. These influences are most apparent in the "people professions" such as psychology, social work, medicine, or teaching, but they extend to other less-obvious areas as well. Scientists work in teams, accountants deal with clients, and historians try to understand past human events. Wherever there are interactions between people, when we try to understand each other, the issues of culture, identity, and intercultural understanding come into play.

The Cultural Identity—Personal and Professional Workshop

Cultural Identity—Personal and Professional is a mandatory workshop for all first-year students in the ACE (Active Collaborative Education[1]), a teacher education program at Kaye College of Education in Beer Sheva, Israel. ACE is a two-year postgraduate program offering teaching certificates for K–12 and special education.

Questions of identity cannot be isolated from other professional questions, and those are discussed in all of our program's components; however, this workshop focuses intentionally on cultural aspects of personal and professional identity and places professional questions within a specific cultural context.

The heterogeneous workshop groups include men and women, Jews, Christian Arabs and Moslem Arabs, recent immigrants and Israeli-born, secular and religious, ages 25–45, single and married, with and without children, from big cities, small towns, and rural areas. In short, our culturally diverse students mirror the composition of Israeli society.

The workshop is based on the following assumptions:

- Our identities are particular and dependent on our social-cultural backgrounds.
- "Identity" is a process of giving meaning and meaningfulness during which individuals come to know their cultural environment and its place in their lives.
- There is a dialectic relationship between the personal and the professional—professional identity development is part of personal identity development and vice-versa.
- Telling personal stories is a tool for both revealing cultural components and forming them.

The work we describe is not about finding our "true self" which is hiding under layers of the unconscious, but an interpretive, dynamic process of learning that creates meaning within a specific cultural context. This process uses materials that come from experiences in the past and the present that are told as stories which, in turn, redesign these experiences (Connelly and Clandinin, 1999; Sfard and Prusak, 2005).

The workshop invites its participants to research their personal culture stories within a community of learners that enables a safe space for intercultural dialogue to take place. This process is not a passive transmission of knowledge from teachers to students, but an active meaning-creation activity in which the students set their own pace and examine the meaning of their cultural profile and the effects it has on the development of their cultural identity. Our purpose is not to bring them to give up their cultural identity, but to be able to see life from more than one perspective, and by doing so, develop intercultural sensitivity.

The Way It Works. Based on an exercise developed by Jane Zeni at the University of Missouri-St. Louis (undated personal communication), the workshop revolves around students' personal stories relating to universal cultural dimensions such as gender, race, generation, place of residence, religion, ethnic heritage, education, class, and family.

Telling stories about our culture helps us become conscious of our experiences, and the ensuing dialogue invites further study and examination of the meaning it bears on who we are. As the stories are told within a multi-cultural environment, the dialogue allows the participants to actually live the experience of being part of a diverse learning community.

Although the meetings are dynamic, and change in response to the needs of the moment, in general, they can be described as a series of "spirals" that emerge from each other:

Story writing—Ten minutes of writing personal stories relating to the specific dimension.

Story sharing—Students tell their stories and others in the group respond by mirroring (which will be explained later) or asking clarifying questions.

Conceptualizing—After hearing several stories the group tries to conceptualize their learning about the specific cultural dimension. For example, in one of the meetings dedicated to the dimension of religion, the following dialogue took place:

> Suhad (a Moslem woman): I'm religious and it seems to me that people who aren't are missing the most important thing in life.
>
> Galit (a Jewish woman): I'm religious too but that doesn't mean that secular people can't be happy.
>
> Suhad: You're religious? But you don't dress like a religious person.
>
> Galit: My belief's in my heart. I don't have to show it.
>
> Suhad: I never thought it possible to be religious without dressing accordingly.

This discussion began with each woman holding a very clear, very different, picture of what it means to be religious. The subsequent group discussion led to a reconceptualization of "religious belief," its many possible meanings and manifestations, a process that enabled the participants to move onto the next stage—re-telling.

Re-telling—The students look back at their own stories, beliefs, and attitudes in light of the stories of the others and the discussion. We call this "your story—my story."

Personal culture article—At the end of the first semester the students write an article on the cultural background that they bring to their work. This personal article tells the student's story through the prisms of three or four dimensions of their choice and includes insights stemming from the processes of telling and discussing "cultural identity stories" in the group. As opposed to the weekly in-class writing, in this article the students put together the cultural mosaic in which they were raised and explore the meanings it has on who they are today and what they bring with them to their professional situations. Students receive extensive feedback on their article but no letter or number grade.

From Personal to Professional. The stories and the written article are not left in a vacuum. The dialectical relationship between the personal and the professional is emphasized when discussions develop around the personal stories and their expression in professional practice. Our experience so far shows that four stages can be identified on the way to understanding and creating the connection between the personal and the professional:

1. *No connection*: Students see their personal lives as irrelevant in the professional context. Most of them start with the perception that the private and the professional should be separate, and there are those who go as far as to say that people who cannot separate the two are not professionals.
2. *Toe-dipping*: Still skeptical, students are prepared to begin examining different aspects of their private life, but they still do not see the connection between their personal stories and learning their profession.
3. *Self-realization*: The connection between the private and the professional begins to show up in their stories.
4. *Integration*: The dialectic relationship between the personal and the professional is recognized. In the following example, an Arab student from the north who works in a Bedouin school in the south commented:

> I started to identify myself within the school, to see the difference between my pupils and myself, in our background, in what each of us believes in and although we're all Moslems, it's different. Although they're pupils, they have something private and special that they believe in. And norms and statuses (different from mine) that I have to deal with and give them a special personal identity. I didn't do that before we worked on this in the workshops. I started to think about the identity of each individual pupil, his economic state, social state, family state, where he lives.

Again, although we saw these stages among teachers-in-training, there is no reason to assume that they are particular only to that specific student population.

Creating a Safe Space for Understanding

Dealing with sensitive issues connected to personal and cultural life experiences necessitates developing an inclusive community that excludes none of its members. Such a community creates a safe space for its participants, a space that fosters trust and a feeling of belonging and neutralizes inhibiting elements such as judgment, stereotyping, inattentiveness, or closing off of the other. This type of space usually does not develop by itself and must be carefully nurtured by its leaders based on the following action principles: participation, non-judgment, legitimacy, and professional connection.

Participation. There can be no lurkers. Participation includes both telling and responding. Each student tells his or her stories, but you must find the setting in which each person feels comfortable. Some students may tell their stories to the whole group, some will tell them only to one or two others, but everyone has a voice and it has to be heard.

Special attention and consideration must be given to questions such as how to help students to choose events and thoughts that they feel comfortable sharing with others and at the same time, allow them to feel free to leave out details that seem too personal to them, or how to encourage them to raise meaningful subjects that will enable them to progress.

Legitimacy. There are no stories that are right or stories that are wrong, no good or bad stories. Stories can be interpreted from different perspectives but every story is legitimate as long as it is authentic.

Non-judgment. Commenting on the stories has to be done in a nonjudgmental way. One way of indicating to the storyteller that we have heard what he is saying is through "mirroring"—returning our understanding of the other's story without judgment, a process that sometimes presents a challenge for the students.

In one year-end discussion, the students stressed the development of the ability to listen to each other, their ability to relate differently to each other, and to communicate beyond the boundaries of religion, nationality, gender, or socio-economic status. By now, they are able to define their learning in a collective ("we") voice: "We learned to live in a complex, heterogeneous group without excluding anyone." In a more personal tone, a Jewish student put it this way:

> I grew up here and I thought I knew the Bedouin culture and suddenly it's different. . . . I was in shock from the things that people described. We argued but it was very fruitful. We shared our experiences and feelings with each other. Even if it came from ignorance, there was no judgment . . . it was legitimate. And through coming to know each other it became legitimate to change your mind.

The "safe place" enables the students to study their developing cultural identity through dialogue within a learning community that plays the part of a "forum of acknowledgement" (White, 1997). As White claims, this public exploration is essential: "Participating in these arenas achieves more than the authentication of a person's knowledgeableness. It is also through these arenas that people can achieve a 'full' or 'thick' description of these knowledges, and of their personal identities" (p. 14).

Glimpses of Understanding: Working with People Who Work with People

Although we have found that one semester (30 hours) provides a good foundation for the work we described above, you do not have to give up on the idea if you cannot devote that much time to it. Shorter versions of the workshop are possible as long as enough time is devoted to building a safe space for the community of learners and there is enough time to experience telling, listening to, and responding to personal culture stories. There are also ways in which different types of personal culture stories can be integrated into almost any class. Although in our workshop we focus on the dimensions mentioned earlier, it is also possible to think in terms of more discipline-specific directions for stories. Here are a few possibilities to start you off:

Literature: Tell a story about reading or being read to as a child. Was reading a solitary or family activity? What book or story do you remember best?

Sciences: Tell a story about how your scientific interest expressed itself (or not) when you were a child. How did your environment (family, school) react to it?

Political science: Tell a story about an election when you were a child. Was politics discussed in your home? Was politics something just for adults or were you involved also?

Use your imagination. Given the fact that any group of learners is de facto multicultural, any personal story can serve as a starting point for developing an attitude appreciative of cultural diversity—an essential ingredient in internationalizing higher education.

An Ethical Perspective

The subject of cultural identity raises ethical questions about what is forbidden and what is permissible, worthwhile or not, possible or blocked. A workshop mainly based on students' personal stories is by its nature dynamic and presents the group with many potential tensions. Some of these tensions and dilemmas were discussed earlier, but there are a few more we would like to open up for further thought.

Encouraging college students to look at their cultural background and explore its influence and significance for the persons they are today has its risks. Are we, as higher education faculty, ready to support those students who stand up and ask difficult questions, who are not happy with what they discover about themselves or their society, who would like to change, but learn that there is very little chance they can? Are we ready to be there for them in those situations, and what are the limits of our readiness, ability, and responsibility to do so?

Despite all of the "safe space" factors mentioned earlier, we must confess that as educators, we do have an agenda. We want our students to express themselves, to tell their stories in public. We want them to ask questions about it and make sense of it. And at the end of the day, we want them to do this whether or not it fits with their personal culture. To what extent do we have the right to do so?

Conclusion

The workshop we described is relevant for everyone, not just for teachers. Who you are as a person cannot and should not be separated from who you are as a professional—it is part of your professional strength.

If you accept this premise, then you must accept our previous argument that working on one's cultural identity should be part of any professional education. We cannot assume that just because we have lived our life, we understand its effects on who we are and what we bring with us to our professional practice. Therefore, the process must work "from the inside out": the personal widens into the professional, the personal cultural understanding widens into understanding the other, and understanding the local other widens into understanding the international other. These ever-widening circles feed back into a deeper understanding of ourselves and the development of intercultural sensitivity.

References

Connelly, F. M., and Clandinin, D. J. (eds.) *Shaping a Professional Identity: Stories of Educational Practice.* New York: Teachers College Press, 1999.

Delpit, L. "The Silenced Dialogue: Power and Pedagogy in Educating Other People's Children." *Harvard Educational Review,* 58(3), 280–298, 1988.

Gallini, J., and Zhang, Y.-L. Socio-cognitive constructs and characteristics of classroom communities: An exploration of relationships. *Journal of Educational Computing Research,* 17(4), 321–339, 1997.

Hobbs, H., and Chernotsky, H. "Preparing Students for Global Citizenship." Paper presented at the American Political Science Association Teaching and Learning Conference, Charlotte, NC, Feb. 9–11, 2007. Retrieved July 22, 2007, from http://www.apsanet.org/tlc2007/TLC07HobbsChernotsky.pdf.

Lurie, Y. *Cultural Beings: Reading the Philosophers of Genesis.* Amsterdam, Netherlands: Rodopi Editions, 2000.

Sfard, A., and Prusak, A. "Telling Identities: In Search of an Analytic Tool for Investigating Learning as a Culturally Shaped Activity." *Educational Researcher,* 34(4), 14–22, 2005.

White, M. (1997). *Narratives of Therapists' Lives.* Adelaide, South Australia: Dulwich Centre Publications.

Note

1. The name of the program, ACE, stands for our educational vision that views learning to become a teacher as being actively engaged within a collaborative community of practice (see http://ceti.macam.ac.il/Courses/shachaf/ace.asp for a short description).

BOBBIE TURNIANSKY *is an organizational psychologist interested in organizational culture and organizational learning and change.*

SMADAR TUVAL *is a school counselor interested in stratification processes in the education system and children's behavioral and emotional disorders.*

RUTH MANSUR *is a philosophy of education scholar interested in the ethic of teaching, multicultural education, and the development of professional identity.*

JUDITH BARAK, *the chair of the ACE program, researches educational change processes and the negotiation of the cultural gap between schools and higher education.*

ARIELA GIDRON *is a narrative researcher with interests in story telling and thinking with metaphors.*

5

Contemplative techniques like meditation can help students to go beyond a merely cognitive understanding of their responsibilities as global citizens, and to find an authentic motivation to serve.

Learning About Obligation, Compassion, and Global Justice: The Place of Contemplative Pedagogy

David Kahane

There are many reasons to internationalize the higher education curriculum: catering to more diverse instructor and student bodies or equipping students to flourish in an increasingly globalized world, for example. For many educators, though, a key reason for internationalization is ethical: it helps students to examine their implicit and explicit beliefs about whose wellbeing matters, and to develop a more globalized sense of responsibility and citizenship. Doing this pedagogical and curricular work, though, raises a set of questions about how those of us in the relatively privileged global north draw boundaries around our concern for others, what motivates our relative indifference to or dissociation from the suffering of distant strangers, and how these dynamics can be challenged and changed. In this chapter, I draw upon my experiences teaching a 300-level philosophy course on "Obligation, Compassion, and Global Justice"[1] to offer a rather unconventional answer to these questions. I suggest that while learning more about global inequalities, reflecting on moral principles, and getting a more vivid sense of the life experiences and perspectives of people in different parts of the world are important to a pedagogy of global citizenship, they are insufficient. A pedagogy of global citizenship also requires that students be supported in contemplative practice, bringing mindful attention to their own embodied experiences of dissociation from their own and others' suffering.

NEW DIRECTIONS FOR TEACHING AND LEARNING, no. 118, Summer 2009 © Wiley Periodicals, Inc.
Published online in Wiley InterScience (www.interscience.wiley.com) • DOI: 10.1002/tl.352

I have taught Philosophy 368 at the University of Alberta in western Canada since 2006, to a class of 35–45 students, about half of them philosophy majors, and half from other disciplines. The course is built around a cognitive and motivational puzzle relating to global citizenship and global justice. The puzzle begins with a few facts:

1. Large numbers of our fellow humans live in abject poverty (1.2 billion, by one recent estimate), go to bed hungry each night (an estimated 800 million people), and die daily from poverty-related causes (perhaps 50,000 a day).
2. We could each prevent a portion of this suffering at minimal cost: the sachet of oral rehydration salts that could save a child from fatal diarrhea costs about fifty cents, and twenty cents buys a day's food rations distributed by the World Food Program in Sudan.
3. Almost all of us who work or study at universities in the global north spend a significant amount on luxuries we could easily forego.

Put these facts together, and a sobering set of choices and trade-offs becomes visible: in drinking lattes rather than regular coffees, for example, I am paying a premium over the course of a year that could instead be used to save many human lives. When I look this equation in the eye, I come to an inexorable conclusion: many aspects of my privilege come at an unconscionable cost, and ought to be given up for the immeasurably greater good that these resources could do for the world's neediest.[2]

This brings us to the puzzle: like most students in my Canadian classrooms, recognizing this obligation changes almost nothing in how I actually live. I manage, like most privileged global citizens, to proceed relatively untroubled in a lifestyle that is unconscionable by my own standards. As decent people, we nonetheless find it hard to take strangers' welfare seriously in making choices, and indeed to hold onto an awareness of others' suffering and our capacity to ameliorate it.

As my own understanding of the dynamics of dissociation from others' suffering developed, the course took on a quite unconventional shape. Before getting to this, I would like to step back and sketch the terrain of approaches to teaching global citizenship, at least from the standpoint of English-speaking political theory.

Pedagogies of Global Citizenship

Only in the last twenty years have mainstream political philosophers in the English-speaking world begun systematically to question the assumption that justice applies only within bounded political communities. Whereas prior to the late 1980s political theorists did not typically even notice that their conceptions of justice screeched to a halt at national borders, debates in political theory now take it as given that many of our deepest challenges of justice (and indeed survival) traverse national boundaries, in a context of profound global interdependence.

Many political theorists now aim to persuade their readers of an individual and collective obligation, on the part of people in the global north, to redress gross inequalities of resources and power with the global south. At an implicit or explicit level, this has these theorists grappling with how to motivate people to recognize and challenge their own privilege, and their own disconnection from the suffering and the fate of those beyond their nation's borders. I see two dominant approaches to motivating change among the privileged.

1. *Pedagogies of reason.* Perhaps unsurprisingly, given the shape of the Western philosophical tradition, the dominant way that English-speaking philosophers have tried to convince their readers to attend to the plight of the world's least well off is through rational argumentation. Peter Singer's (1997) influential argument—which I used to set up the puzzle above—provides a clear example of this resort to rational persuasion as a route to changing self-perceptions, understandings of obligation, and ultimately behavior on the part of the privileged. Singer's argument is premised on the view that morality requires impartial fairness between people, and that from an impartial standpoint, the gross disparities in wealth and life prospects across the globe are morally indefensible. He suggests that almost all of us are impartialist in our deepest moral convictions, but that we self-servingly ignore the entailments of this in our everyday behavior, treating the satisfaction of our most casual desires as more important than meeting the crucial needs of strangers. The role of the philosopher is to point out this sharp contradiction between our moral convictions and our behavior, so that we can see our own hypocrisy and, hopefully, be moved to reduce the conflict.

   Yet, as I have observed in my own life and my own classrooms, being rationally persuaded of a moral obligation is rarely effective in motivating change. Nor does the resilience of our privileged modes of behavior seem adequately explained by hypocrisy or weakness of the will, concepts that describe the dictates of morality being outweighed by our nonmoral or immoral preferences, goals, or desires. Rather, the "knowing" that we achieve through exposure to rational arguments about obligation seems disconnected from the complexity even of our moral being, and is eroded or displaced not by desire or by conscious, countervailing goals, but by complicated dynamics of dissociation and motivation.

2. *Pedagogies of sentiment.* A number of prominent philosophers now argue that acting ethically toward others is less a matter of applying abstract moral principles than of learning about the particularities of others' lives, and so developing empathy and compassion for them. Richard Rorty (1993), for example, suggests that the main obstacle to

our offering help to distant strangers is that they don't seem like part of a valued "we." This isn't remedied, though, through abstract, principled argumentation; rather, it's through vehicles like literature that our sense of the boundaries of our moral communities can shift. We hear sad, sentimental stories about others' suffering, and suddenly see that they are mothers like us, or get their hearts broken like us, or love soccer like us. Out of these particular realizations comes a sense of connection and commitment that can change our behavior.

Martha Nussbaum (1996a, 1996b) offers a different kind of therapy of sentiment: she suggests that when we learn about the particularity of others' lives, we are able to see that they share a variety of distinctively human capacities with us, and so deserve our regard. This is not merely an abstract realization, but a cultivation of both reason and passion that expands our circle of concern. So she describes a cosmopolitan education, one that involves learning how distant communities and cultures live, and increases our sense of appreciation for otherness, and our commitment to global citizenship.

Pedagogies of sentiment seem to offer a more promising diagnosis of our dissociation from the suffering of distant strangers than do pedagogies of reason, for they offer a more complex picture of the learner. But pedagogies of sentiment do not quite account for the cognitive and motivational puzzle that I laid out earlier: internationalizing the classroom and giving students plenty of particularistic information about other countries and groups does not in fact seem to displace habits of privilege, nor does it seriously diminish dissociation from others' suffering.

I would suggest that our dissociation from others' suffering is persistent because it is powerfully motivated—not by self-interest, as pedagogies of reason might suggest, but by inchoate fear. This, at least, is what I discover when I attend closely to my own experience, say when a charity infomercial appears on my TV with the image of a starving child: a wave of sensation and emotion flashes through me, a hint of my visceral belief that if I let this suffering in (not to mention the countless reiterations of this suffering in further starving children), it will destroy me. And another discovery when I attend closely to my own experience: that this recoiling from others' suffering has a counterpart in my relationship to my own suffering. Here too, I withdraw and dissociate from emotional intensity, out of a visceral conviction that I cannot stand to experience it unmediated. One further discovery: that a tremendous number of my habits, including habits of consumption, serve to soothe and deaden the anxiety that arises from a fear of directly experiencing suffering—others' and my own.

My point is not that this story of my own dissociation from suffering and habits of privilege is precisely mirrored in your experience or that of my students. Rather, the point is that this "deeper" story of my motivations and resistances, of my embodied and emotional experiences, is so much at odds with the narrative I would standardly offer of my life, my moral and philosophical commitments, and the kind of person I am. I suggest, in other words, that just as we spend much of our privileged lives disconnected from the suffering of strangers, so we spend them caught up in narratives and self-descriptions that do a poor job of describing the reality of our embodied experience. This is the most profound element of our alienation: alienation from the reality of our internal worlds. This is not an alienation that gets corrected by rational reflection or by a rich sense of the particulars of others' lives.

This alienation gets corrected, I want to suggest, by the ability to observe our own present-moment experience with a certain degree of compassionate detachment. This compassionate self-observation of our own bodily sensations and emotional patterns requires an ability to let the usual storylines go to begin to notice what is going on in us right now. This sort of rigorous yet kind self-observation gets learned through ongoing practice, through a form of inquiry seldom used in the contemporary western academy: contemplation.

Contemplative Pedagogy

Both pedagogies of reason and pedagogies of sentiment tend to remain within a paradigm of education and scholarship as third-person knowing. Our subject matter—principles of moral obligation, facts about global interdependence, narratives about the lives of others, facts about the psychology of dissociation and by-standing—lies outside of us, and we use careful analysis and critical reflection to reach understanding, and to orient our actions in the world.

The puzzle with which Philosophy 368 begins is that of the entrenchment of habits of privilege. Neither more information nor more careful rational reflection are able to shift our deep patterns of thought, affect, or experience. We may feel empathy for others' suffering, or connection to distant others, as we learn more about them, but these changes tend to remain superficial and evanescent so long as we neglect a first-person realization of the powerful motivations and drives that underlie our persistent tendency to dissociate. This, at least, is the analysis that led me to complement third-person approaches in Philosophy 368 with the first-person inquiry of contemplative pedagogy.

Contemplative pedagogy is getting increasing attention in North American higher education: a yearly week-long workshop began at Smith College in 2005, attracting about 40 educators to each summer session,[3] and Naropa University initiated its own international summer session on contemplative pedagogy in 2007[4]; a major international conference was held on the subject at Columbia University Teachers College in 2005[5] and another in San Francisco in 2007.[6] Even the staid *Chronicle of Higher Education* has reported positively on the movement (Gravois, 2005). Contemplative pedagogies include a wide range of practices, but the orienting practice and experience is that of meditation. As Arthur Ledoux (1998) writes,

> By meditation I mean the practice of mindfulness, training the mind to focus
> in a steady and non-judging way on the different phases of human experience.
> Mindfulness is an ancient practice cultivated strongly in Buddhist traditions
> but which overlaps contemplative practices in many other traditions. Mind-
> fulness practice typically begins by paying clear, steady, non-reactive atten-
> tion to the sensations of one's own breathing and then extending this wise
> and compassionate attention to embrace all bodily sensations and then feel-
> ings, moods, thoughts, and intentions. One way to describe the goal of mind-
> fulness is the cultivation of bare attention: the ability to focus on any aspect
> of life whatsoever with this calm concentration (see http://www.bu.edu/
> wcp/Papers/Teac/TeacLedo.htm).

The goal of the contemplative pedagogies that I introduced in Philosophy
368 was to cultivate this kind of mindfulness.

Contemplative Techniques in Philosophy 368. Implementing contemplative pedagogies in my course on global justice felt like a dangerous
leap: I had been developing my own meditation practice for only a couple
of years and though I saw important implications for studying and teaching about compassion and obligation toward the global poor, I was uncertain about how to realize these. How, for example, should I present the
relationship between contemplative pedagogies and the conventional forms
of inquiry associated with the discipline of philosophy? I eventually realized that I did not have to resolve these tough pedagogical questions outside of the course itself; rather, the course could itself constitute a collective
inquiry into the significance of contemplation to the issues we were studying. In this and many other respects, bringing contemplation into my pedagogies marked a seismic shift in my teaching practice: it led me to give up
a great deal of control and authority in my classroom, and to invite students
to be conscious participants in pedagogical reflection. Let me outline three
major contemplative elements of the course.

Meditation. In every meeting of the class, we did about seven minutes of
mindfulness meditation, calmly focusing our attention on the movement
of our breath (noticing the sensation of the breath, counting breaths), and
returning to our breath each time we noticed ourselves getting caught up in
thoughts. I was careful in explaining the rationale for meditation practice as
part of the course, but offered quite spare instructions for the practice itself.
I would remind students to sit up straight in their seats, feet flat on the floor,
arms comfortable on their laps or tables. I would remind them that the goal
was not to stop themselves from thinking, but rather to notice when they got
lost in thoughts: the core of the practice was then to let thoughts go and
return to the breath, over and over again. I would remind them of the importance of kindness toward themselves when they noticed they were thinking:
this was not a contest, but a rigorously gentle exploration of our own experience. After some feedback and experimentation, we decided that this period
of meditation worked best if placed right at the start of class; students were

good at arriving on time and if they did not, they would wait outside until the bell that signaled the end of meditation.

I had anticipated student resistance to meditating in class, imagining that some students would judge it a waste of time, or irrelevant to the course's subject matter, or unphilosophical. Instead, students were almost uniformly enthusiastic about it. Based on formative and summative feedback from students, at least four things happened. First, most students deeply appreciated the chance to simply slow down. They spent their days rushing from class to class, juggling intense demands associated with school and jobs, bombarded with images and sounds; and they cherished the opportunity simply to do nothing for seven minutes. Second, many appreciated not only the break, but the practice of contemplation: they were curious about their internal lives, and interested in training themselves to notice their in-the-moment experience in new ways. Third, they were able to see connections of meditation to the course material, and interested in meditatively exploring their relationship to suffering and moral responsibility. This was helped along by the use of a text, read across the term and alongside more philosophical articles, that discussed themes of contemplation and our relationship to our own and others' suffering (Dass and Gorman, 1988). In general, the first-person elements of the course invited students to bring the sometimes arcane arguments of philosophers into dialogue with their own experience, and offered them a rigorous set of techniques that supported this. And fourth, meditating together at the beginning of each class brought us into the room together, and allowed a calmer and more careful engagement with one another; this laid the foundation for better work in groups than students were used to experiencing, or than I had ever experienced in other classrooms.

Free-writing. It was at the 2005 Summer Session on Contemplative Curriculum Design that I came to recognize, through a presentation by Mary Rose O'Reilley, that free-writing could be understood as a contemplative practice (see O'Reilley, 1993). Free-writing, popularized by Peter Elbow (1973), means writing without stopping for a fixed period of time—the only rule is that the pen not stop moving. Because writing in this way short-circuits the impulse to edit, it allows writing without so much scripting and conscious control; one gets into the flow of an idea or impulse, and writes things that one didn't know one had to say.

I offered a prompt or question for each free-write. Several times during the term, free-writes followed meditation, allowing for students to process that experience. Other times, free-writes invited reflection on a particular text, or a question that we had been struggling with in discussion up to that moment.

Sometimes, when the topic of a free-write was very raw, I would let students know in advance that they would not be asked to share the writing or to include it in their portfolio. The default, though, was for the free-write to be submitted, returned by me with only a "thank you" as a comment or evaluation, and then included in their portfolio. Sometimes, students would be asked to read their free-writes to one another in small groups, and here we followed a protocol that I learned from O'Reilley. Writers would be given a couple of minutes to decide if there were elements of their writing that they wished to leave out when they read. Then each student would read their work to their peers, who would listen as mindfully as they could, and simply say "thank you" at the end and on to the next reading without further discussion.

Free-writing not only offered a mode of contemplative inquiry, but also helped to alleviate some of the anxiety and intimidation that students experience around writing. I was astounded again and again by the wisdom and authenticity of voice that I encountered in just about every free-write—a much rarer phenomenon when I read students' analytical essays. I also believe that free-writing, together with other low-stakes writing exercises used in the course, helped students to grasp that writing is a way of generating thoughts, and not only of representing thoughts that have already been nailed down.

Lectio Divina. Another technique that I took from O'Reilley was *lectio divina,* or sacred reading, which has its origins in the Catholic monastic tradition. For a fixed period—perhaps five minutes—students would focus on an assigned paragraph of text, and would try to bring the mind of meditation to their reading. Rather than following thoughts about the text, they would try to dwell on it simply, reading repeatedly whatever aspects caught their eye, and seeing what meanings emerged. Underlining was permitted, but not note taking. We also applied this technique to photographs—in the very first class of term, for example, students moved from meditation to four minutes of contemplation of a photograph of a man cradling a starving child.

Following this contemplative reading or seeing, students might be asked to free-write to capture what had come to them, or simply to talk in groups about the experience. Students frequently expressed surprise at the meanings that they stumbled across in this way, and the connections they were able to make. Like free-writing, *lectio divina* suspended some of students' intimidation and self-monitoring, and allowed them to tap into new levels of meaning, experience, and insight. Some students also expressed appreciation for the atmosphere of awe, or at least care, that contemplative reading brought to the written word: it cultivated an ethos of intellectual engagement that can be lost in the speed and instrumentality of much university reading.

Outcomes. I taught this contemplative version of Philosophy 368 in 2006 and 2007, and will teach it again in 2008. Student responses have been enthusiastic, as conveyed through anonymous formative evaluations conducted several times each term, and through narrative comments and numerical results on formal summative evaluations.[7] Stepping back from details, I would observe four things about outcomes.

First, student reactions made clear to me their thirst for courses that allow them to engage with their own experiences in rigorous and reflective ways, and to think carefully about questions of meaning, morality, and spirituality in their lives.[8] There is a useful distinction to be made, though, between contemplative pedagogies (which train students in particular approaches to self-observation) and holistic education (which can more easily invite students to tell their habitual stories about themselves, rather than directing mindful attention to what is beneath these stories). I find echoes of this distinction in students' comments on the course, where a number of them note a difference between the kind of personal perspective they were encouraged to develop in this course, and invitation in other courses to "share their feelings" or "speak from their perspective" (which some of them described as irrelevant and/or infantilizing).

Second, student feedback indicated a deepened interest in issues of global justice, and in their own implication in global injustice. Many students indicated that they remained puzzled about their ethical responsibilities and about the dynamics of dissociation and compassion that the course had taken up; but to me this uncertainty is a fruitful one, and often was held by students with real curiosity, as well as gentleness toward themselves. Students tended to move away from harsh judgments of themselves and others for implication in global injustice—away from a discourse of obligation and guilt that I believe distracts from our tendency or even ability to connect compassionately with those in need. They tended to move toward a willingness to experiment with their own tolerance for letting in others' suffering, and with what this might feel like in action. And they tended to be increasingly open to the possibility that their service to those who suffered, whether by giving up luxuries for others, or volunteering, or reorienting career and life plans, might not be a sacrifice (as Peter Singer suggests), but rather a movement toward greater meaning and fulfillment in their lives.

Third, the overtly experimental quality of the course, and the amount of uncertainty we entertained together about both method and content, seemed to cultivate a less anxious, more curious, even delighted stance toward learning. Narrative evaluation comments repeatedly said that for a course about such depressing subject matter, it really was engaging and fun. My analysis here is that in much of their educational experience, students are reminded repeatedly of what they lack, and come to treat education as a treadmill to gain praise and avoid humiliation. A range of aspects of this course—from the emphasis on compassion toward self that is part of meditation, to the cultivation of trust among students in the classroom, to the pervasive spirit of inquiry in the course—opened up for students a sense that they might in fact learn from a place of plenty, where they have genuine knowledge to offer one another, and where there's collective pleasure in exploring tough questions.

Fourth, the sense of operating from a place of plenty rather than lack, and so experiencing genuine curiosity and joy in learning, characterized my own experience of the course. Because I made the tentativeness and experimental quality of the course methods explicit to students and invited them to be agents in this inquiry, I was freed to be uncertain, and so to be a learner in my own classroom. Because I would do classroom exercises alongside my students, I got to explore my own present-moment experience of teaching (and of inquiring into the issues of the course) through meditation and free-writing, in ways that changed my sense of my experience and possibilities as a teacher. The community, the curiosity, and the mutual support that we built in the classroom, in part thanks to contemplative methods, included me as well: I ended up experiencing and modeling the freedom in learning that I sought for my students that I now realize I was yearning for in my own experience of the classroom.

Issues and Future Directions

The contemplative principles and practices described in this chapter are being used across disciplines and institutions, from poetry courses at West Point to physics courses at Amherst College. Nevertheless, there are distinctive issues that arise with contemplative pedagogies, some of which continue to confront me.

First, there is an issue that I have not faced at all, but that I gather looms over the use of contemplative pedagogies in U.S. contexts: the question of the legitimacy or even permissibility of bringing spiritual practices into the classroom, especially in public colleges and universities. There is a ready answer to this question, in that meditation is increasingly accepted as a thoroughly secular practice—taught, for example, in medical contexts to reduce stress and mitigate pain. However, in the contemplative pedagogy community, there is another side to this coin of secularization: meditation techniques have their roots in rich Buddhist and Muslim and Jewish and Christian traditions, and there might be a loss in stripping away these spiritual contexts to popularize contemplation, including as a pedagogy.

Second, I face questions of the experience and adeptness I should have with a contemplative practice before I introduce it in the classroom. I struggled with this in introducing simple mindfulness meditation, and struggle with it again as I look ahead to the next iteration of the course, where I plan to experiment with *metta,* or loving kindness meditation. My response to this uncertainty has been to go ahead—to embrace the shakiness I may feel in this aspect of my teaching (as in many others), and to let students be participants in assessing what works. What seems crucial is that I myself be practicing mindfulness and presence as best I can while teaching contemplative techniques (rather than having my attention elsewhere, or being caught up in fantasies or stories about what is going on). There also is a crucial distinction between employing contemplative pedagogies, and seeking to be a spiritual teacher; in the context of the academy, the former must not be allowed to slide over into the latter.

A colleague recently shared a gem of advice about teaching meditation that came from Chogyam Trungpa, the Tibetan Buddhist teacher, and that provides a provocative and challenging baseline for contemplative pedagogies: the requirement is that while you are actually teaching meditation, you remain sane. I am working at this.

A third issue that I continue to struggle with is around contemplative and analytical modes of writing. I noted above the liveliness of spontaneous student writing, and the labored and intimidated quality of much analytical writing. I desperately want to understand more about how I can support my students in writing analytically from a place of plenty rather than lack, as well as in finding a more authentic voice as philosophical writers.

A final issue has become more and more vivid to me as I have ventured into fresh territory in my teaching: how much the success of different pedagogies indexes to my ability to be present and grounded in offering them. This does not mean certainty that they will work; indeed, presence and groundedness often feels inquisitive, and even uncertain. However, as I learn to bring contemplation more fully into my own life, and my own in teaching, I gain a sense of what it means to be authentic in my role as teacher, and to hold this seat with the authority of someone who is not hiding from himself.

Contemplative pedagogies, I have suggested, can help students to understand the habits of thought, judgment, and reaction that keep them trapped in the cocoon of their own privilege, which is also to say their own suffering. As such, these pedagogies have a pivotal role to play in internationalizing higher education, insofar as one goal of internationalization is to cultivate a meaningful and motivating sense of global citizenship. I hope I have also made clear, though, that contemplative pedagogies deepen the process of teaching and learning much more pervasively than this: they bring our bare humanity into the classroom in ways that allow education to be more holistic, more fulfilling, and more real for both professors and students.[9]

References

Dass, R., and Gorman, P. *How Can I Help? Stories and Reflections on Service.* New York: Alfred A. Knopf, 1988.

Elbow, P. *Writing Without Teachers.* Oxford: Oxford University Press, 1973.

Gravois, J. "Meditate on It: Can Adding Contemplation to the Classroom Lead Students to More Eureka Moments?" *The Chronicle of Higher Education*, October 21, 2005, 52(9), A10. Retrieved October 19, 2007, from http://chronicle.com/free/v52/i09/09a01001.htm

Ledoux, A. O. "Teaching Meditation to Classes in Philosophy." Paper presented at Twentieth World Congress of Philosophy, Boston, 1998. Retrieved October 16, 2007, from http://www.bu.edu/wcp/Papers/Teac/TeacLedo.htm

Nussbaum, M. "Patriotism and Cosmopolitanism." In M. Nussbaum and J. Cohen (eds.), *For Love of Country: Debating the Limits of Patriotism.* Boston: Beacon Press, 1996a.

Nussbaum, M. "Compassion: The Basic Social Emotion." *Social Philosophy and Policy*, 13(1), 27–58, 1996b.

O'Reilley, M. R. *The Peaceable Classroom.* Portsmouth, NH: Boynton/Cook, 1993.

Pogge, T. *World Poverty and Human Rights: Cosmopolitan Responsibilities and Reforms.* Cambridge: Polity Press, 2002.

Rorty, R. "Human Rights, Rationality, and Sentimentality." In S. Shute and S. Hurley (eds.), *On Human Rights: The Oxford Amnesty Lectures 1993.* New York: Basic Books, 1993.
Singer, P. "Famine, Affluence, and Morality." In H. LaFollette (ed.), *Ethics in Practice: An Anthology.* Oxford: Blackwell, 1997.
Unger, P. *Living High and Letting Die: Our Illusion of Innocence.* Oxford: Oxford University Press, 1996.

Notes

1. For the course syllabus, see http://www.arts.ualberta.ca/phil368/2007-368-Syllabus.pdf
2. There are a range of well-worn ripostes to this argument (e.g., saving children from starvation only leads to more suffering down the line); these ripostes are canvassed and rather effectively demolished in Pogge (2002) and Unger (1996).
3. This summer session is convened by the Center for the Contemplative Mind in Society, and funded by the Fetzer Foundation. See http://www.contemplativemind.org/programs/academic/
4. See http://www.naropa.edu/cace/seminar.cfm
5. See http://www.contemplativemind.org/programs/academic/05conference.html
6. See http://www.heartofeducation.org/
7. In 2006, median ratings on a five-point scale included "In-class time was used effectively" = 4.5; "I am motivated to learn more about these subject areas" = 4.8; "I increased my knowledge of the subject areas in this course" = 4.8; "Overall, the quality of the course content was excellent" = 4.7; "The instructor provided constructive feedback throughout the course" = 4.9; and "Overall, this instructor was excellent" = 4.9. All of these results are above the 75th percentile, and many of them are above the 90th percentile.
8. This impression is supported by research results from the Spirituality in Higher Education project, led by Alexander and Helen Astin at UCLA. The extensive, U.S.-based survey found, for example, that 76% of college students say they are "searching for meaning and purpose in life," whereas more than half say that their professors never provide opportunities to discuss the meaning and purpose of life. See http://www.spirituality.ucla.edu.
9. My thanks to the Center for the Contemplative Mind in Society and to Naropa University for their respective seminars in contemplative pedagogy; to the Fetzer Foundation and the Frederick P. Lenz Foundation for funding these seminars; to the University of Alberta for supporting and recognizing my experiments in contemplative pedagogy; and to Susan Burgraff, Meena Gupta, Cressida Heyes, Judith Simmer-Brown, and Danielle Taschereau-Mamers for many rich discussions of the topics in this chapter.

DAVID KAHANE *is an associate professor of political science and Vargo Distinguished Teaching Chair at the University of Alberta.*

6

Instead of treating internationalization as the addition of multicultural elements to a Western curriculum, why not begin with a non-Western curriculum framework?

The Sattvic Curriculum: A Three-Level, Non-Western, Superstructure for Undergraduate Education

Martin Haigh

Introduction

Internationalization of the curriculum usually involves bolting multicultural elements onto a wholly Western foundation (Dale and Robertson, 2003). Often, this process is scripted by the presumption that Western liberal norms shall prevail and that many international learners need remedial instruction in Western culture and thought (Sidhu, 2003; Stier, 2004). However, internationalization should be more than "them learning from us" (Stier, 2004). Many non-Western cultures are vital living traditions. They contain much that is positive. We should use these resources in the internationalization of our much criticized educational system and be open to useful ideas from outside (Berry, 1999; Orr, 1994). If not, then let us recognize that, really, we do not mean to "internationalize the curriculum" at all, but merely to create a more inclusive Western-style education.

Of course, if we were to make changes, a good place to begin might be at the top. Therefore, I offer you an illustration, a viable and easily accessible whole curriculum superstructure grown from completely non-Western stocks. This model has respectable origins in classical philosophy. It is simple, easy to understand, and easily implemented (because it is not such a

NEW DIRECTIONS FOR TEACHING AND LEARNING, no. 118, Summer 2009   © Wiley Periodicals, Inc.
Published online in Wiley InterScience (www.interscience.wiley.com) • DOI: 10.1002/tl.353

great shift from what is done at present in Western higher education institutions). However, it is timely because it promotes the subtle change of direction that is required by the educations for planetary citizenship and a sustainable future advocated by the United Nations' Decade of Education for Sustainable Development (2005–2014; UNESCO, 2004). Hopefully, the system will be pioneered by my Department, but after three conference presentations to more general audiences, I am beginning to get a feel for the qualms of those who are reluctant to consider the challenge of moving beyond their Eurocentric traditions, and some of their objections are described.

The Three Modes of Nature

Samkhya has been called "the most ancient and the most perfect system of positive philosophy" (Ramakrishnananda, 1949, p. 14). In common with most other systems of Indian philosophy, it recognizes that consciousness, not materiality, is the foundation of all understanding. It proceeds by reconstructing the human world through enumeration of the qualities that emerge from the interactions between conscious spirit (Purusa) and material nature (Prakriti; Larson, 1979). These are expressed in terms of three qualities, modes, or, more literally, strands. These are the three "Gunas," which are widely known because they are used heavily by the *Bhagavadgita,* a text sometimes caricatured as the *Hindu New Testament* (Tapasyananda, 1984). However, similar notions are also employed by Classical Yoga and, in less potent forms, by Nyaya-Vaisiseka, Vedanta, Buddhist, and Jain Philosophy (Ramakrishna Rao, 1963). In addition, the Gunas play major practical roles in the Ayurvedic system of medicine and in Indian psychometric analysis (Arulmani, 2007; Johari, 2000; Wolf, 1999).

The three Gunas are *Sattva,* which means light and shining; *Rajas,* which means stimulating and active; and *Tamas,* which means heavy and enveloping. The classical text, the fourth century *Samkhyakarika,* explains that the Gunas characterize everything, both manifest and un-manifest, and that everything can be explained in terms of the relative balance between these three factors (Isvarakrishna, verses 9–14, in Larson, 1979). However, I think their role is most easily explained through the analogy of a color photograph album. This may contain many pictures, but whatever their subject, be it Jordan or Jaipur, all are produced from the ink of just three primary colors, mixed in different proportions. Similarly, everything in the material world is created from the three Gunas: Sattva, Rajas, and Tamas in different combinations. Sattva contributes every aspect that is light, sentient, serene, harmonious and peaceful; Rajas: active, dynamic, creative, destructive, and changing; Tamas: immobile, inert, dark, banal, heavy, negating, and veiled.

Yes, these Gunas characterize everything, for example, food. Sattvic foods are fresh, juicy, nourishing, sweet, and sustain the body without stress (e.g., fresh fruits, vegetables, fresh milk and butter, sprouted beans, grains, pulses).

Rajasic foods are spicy, salty, pungent, sour, or hot and engage passion or stress (e.g., fried food, curry, shellfish, meat). Tamasic foods are lazy, boring, tasteless, heavily processed, narcotic, and/or unhealthy (e.g., anything in a can, "instant," snack pack, red meat, and alcohol; Johari, 2000). They apply to each intention; Sattva rests mindfully in this moment now, Rajas is future "going to . . ." oriented, while Tamas is grumpily past oriented. They also apply to everything done. For example, suppose I wish to make an image of Gaia, the Greek Goddess of the Earth, for my environment course. First, I collect some clay. This is inert Tamasic, formless, an obstacle to overcome just like my feeling, "oh, I can't be bothered." However, Rajas, creative energy, bounds enthusiastically to my rescue; I envision the final outcome and, so inspired, set to work. Finally, success, my image of the Goddess is claimed from the mud. In contemplation, She is serene, beautiful, and together we are Sattvic (Prabhavananda and Isherwood, 1944). Throughout this process, those three Gunas compete for supremacy. Sometimes Rajas drives me forward, overpowering Sattvic contemplation and Tamasic indolence with creative urgency. Sometimes, despondent, Tamas drags me down and both Sattva and Rajas dissipate in blank gloom. Sometimes, Sattva transcends and both Rajas and Tamas are subordinated to warm creative imagination.

As you see, the Gunas contain an evolutionary sequence. Cosmogenesis, as envisaged by the mediaeval Siddhanta Darasanam of Vyasa (3.1–4; Sandal, 1925), begins with Sattva, which is pure possibility, then from Rajas comes intellect, will power, the spirit of creation and finally, third, from Tamas comes possessive egotism. In human terms, well, we are all born in ignorance, Tamas, but as we mature, we gain knowledge through experience and engagement with the world, Rajas. Eventually, we begin to wonder what all this is about and through reflection and introspection seek an integrated understanding of the big picture, Sattva. In the same way, in the West's "Deep Ecology," a core Green philosophy, self-development proceeds through the recognition of the Personal Self, then the larger Social Self and, finally, to the recognition of an Ecological Self, which contains the Deep Ecologist's intuition that humans are a part of Nature (Naess, 1987). Of course, here in the West, "self activity . . . has been a name for the ultimate educational ideal" (Dewey, 1939, p. 602).

The Sattvic Curriculum

Because the Gunas condition every action, inevitably, this includes the understanding and education of learners. In fact, this is described by Sri Krishna in the philosophical discourse that is the *Bhagavadgita* (18. 20–22; Prabhupada, 1972; Tapasyananda, 1984). Tamas, of course, inertia and mindlessness, discourages learners from thought or study and allows only lazy surface learning. To overcome Tamas, it is necessary to become motivated, to think, aspire, and act. Rajas is about action and engagement; it promotes analysis and the development of skills, but it also encourages learners to classify, to focus on things in separation and see them as resources. To move beyond Rajas, it is necessary to move beyond thoughts of possession and beyond seeing the world as a collection of separate things with names and forms. Sattva encourages learners to see things as a whole; it promotes synthesis, holistic learning. The Sattvic perspective embraces the underlying unity that governs everything.

So, the three Gunas suggest a three-level curriculum. Level 1 deals with the obstacle of dispelling Tamas, removing ignorance, inertia, and building the self-motivational base of constructive action. Swami Vivekananda says that, "Education is the manifestation of the perfection already in Humans. Therefore, the only duty of the teacher . . . is to remove all obstructions from the way" (Vivekananda, 1894, in Vivekananda, 1989, v4, p. 358).

Obstructions overcome, level 2 becomes devoted to Rajas and tapping the inherent creativity, energy, and passion within each learner. Again, Vivekananda advocates, "set yourselves to dig the earth . . . by discovering new avenues to production, by your own exertions aided by Western science . . . be full of activities" Vivekananda (1899, in Vivekananda, 1989, v7, p. 183). In the same way, Rabindranath Tagore would cast each learner as a world-worker, a *visvakarman*, who acts for the welfare of all, present and future, and who demonstrates the "union of education and life" (Tagore, 1930, p. 42; Tagore, 1961, p. 43).

Finally, actions completed, work done, at level 3 the learner could move on to Sattvic reflection, philosophy, ethics, synthesis, and overview, perhaps through application of Sri Aurobindo's three learning processes: widening— the broadening of perspectives, deepening—seeing within oneself and beneath the surface of material affairs, and heightening—seeing oneself in context, self-less and free of personal chauvinisms (Huppes, 2001).

Of course, this pattern maps quite neatly across the familiar structures of Anglo-American undergraduate education. Obviously, it is difficult to generalize, but my experience in geography and her sister disciplines and as a member of several other course planning committees suggest that the pattern chimes with curricular forms. So, recast into crude practice, education at level 1 would involve helping learners comprehend facts, lore, and skills, not necessarily passively but without much unconstrained creativity. This would correspond to the Introduction courses typical of a UK undergraduate first year or 100–200 levels in the American system. This basic training would, for many programs, set the scene for creative action in level 2, which might involve active learning, research, analysis, problem solving, critical evaluation, and classification of the world into names, processes, concepts, and forms, perhaps with a view to intervention in worldly affairs (Jackson and Shaw, 2006). Level 2 would emphasize exploration, learning how to do things, and might contain courses entitled "Management . . . ," "Conservation . . . ," "Research . . . ," or "Critical . . ." that correspond to a typical UK undergraduate's second and early third year program or to 300 level courses and up in the United States. The highest level, level 3, would be devoted to Sattvic activities such as philosophy, reflection, overview, and synthesis, where learners are encouraged to develop deeper ethical and empathic understandings, a holistic overview, and perhaps see their education, work, lives, and future as a single whole. In the British system, such synoptic courses are typical of the later stages of the third year, while in the United States, they are common in the level 500 courses that often presage and introduce master's training (see Table 6.1).

"Ah Yes, but . . . ": Some Frequently Asked Questions. "Gunas, fine, but this structure, isn't it pretty much what we are doing already?" The question has cropped up in all three of the public airings of this notion and the answer is "yes" and that is half of its beauty. This scheme could be adopted without doing much to change existing structures or to disturb educational leaders and policy makers.

Of course, its impacts are subtle. Sooner or later, the principles of this internationalized curriculum would begin to affect everything conducted in its name, for while this theoretical framework provides for the same things that many educators already try to achieve, its goals more overtly concern the development of the learner's spiritual self (Milojevic, 2005). It embeds notions, like those proposed by Mahatma Gandhi, that the highest form of learning is based not upon competitive advancement at all costs, but on the self-realization of personal potential and harmonious service to the well-being of all (Kumarappa, 1945). All this is excellent in terms of those educations for citizenship and sustainable development, but nonsense in the language of commerce and materialism (Haigh, 2008). However, many may agree that education means more than just training for the workplace (Berry, 1999).

"So you discuss what this structure would mean for the three levels but you do so in rather general terms . . . but again, it's unclear what really needs to change." The answer is the minds, of instructor and learner alike. The Sattvic Curriculum engages a different mindset. Like Yoga, it subordinates content and competitive achievement to its goal of self-development.

A decade ago, Jacques Delors (1996) proposed an education based on four pillars. First was *learning to know*—building the learning skills needed to comprehend the world and attain the joy that grows from understanding, here: dispelling Tamas. Second was *learning to do*, which involved building the personal skills needed to interact with people, solve problems, and advance understanding, here: engaging Rajas. Third was *learning to live together*, which involved service in common projects designed to help build an appreciation of the interdependence and value of all beings, and fourth was *learning to be*, the integrated development of mind, body, intelligence, sensitivity, aesthetic appreciation, and spirituality—together: Sattva.

The Sattvic Curriculum presents all this as a developmental sequence. In practice, at each level, it requires courses that are constructively aligned to each evolutionary goal: knowledge—basic skills and energy; action—constructive creativity, focus, and ultimately, awareness of context; then finally,

Table 6.1. Outline for the Sattvic Curriculum

Three Levels of the Sattvic Curriculum	Aim "What you hope to achieve"	Curriculum "What you need to do"	Strategies "How you can do it"	Techniques "Tools you could use"
1. Dispelling Tamas (Motivational)	To remove the inertia, lack of confidence, and absence of motivation that inhibits learning and provide the skills needed to progress.	Emphasize inspirational and enthusiasm-building activity supported by the teaching of useful knowledge and accessible methods, all underpinned by the positive reinforcement of learner self-belief.	Establish the basics and encouragement engagement by positive feedback, e.g., invitational practices (Purkey and Stanley, 1991).	Knowledge-based tests, quizzes, posters, simple practical exercises, and student-led spoken presentations, such as debates and role plays.
2. Engaging Rajas (Building skills, experience, and self-confidence)	To build learner creativity and self-confidence as a practitioner and to build experience that may be the subject of later reflection.	Emphasize learner exploration, research-skills, inquiry-based problem-solving, and practical exercises.	Encouragement and development of practical experience supported by a progressive transition toward learner-led and defined creative explorations (e.g., Jackson and Shaw, 2006).	Project reports, written and spoken, direct field experience, laboratory experimentation, questionnaire surveys, classification, analysis, critical analysis of sources and schools, etc., often engaging teamwork.
3. Reflecting Sattva (Building perspective, self-awareness, and empathy for others)	To encourage the learner to see the bigger picture, to set what they are doing in context, and consider their own actions and duties.	Emphasize synthesis, reflection on practice, empathic and ethical awareness.	Encouragement of reflective practice and philosophical insights through the exploration of implications and consequences, ethical dilemmas, conflict resolution, and service learning.	Synoptic overviews, exploring ethical and philosophical problems, as through reflective learning diaries and portfolios.

integration—overview, empathy, reflection, philosophy, and ethics. Each level suggests different styles of instruction, exercise, and assessment. However, if you would like these explored in detail, you will need to read the book length version of this article (Haigh, 2009).

"If the first year should be directed at overcoming inertia and surface learning, etc. (Tamas), what does that mean for practice?" It means the instructors' task is to inform, engage, enthuse, if you will, to invite learning (Purkey and Stanley, 1991).

"Why is it that anything 'Sattvic' can only be introduced in level three?" The Gunas color everything, but in different combinations. All three Gunas affect every course. All that shifts between levels is the emphasis. For example, it is difficult to engage in Sattvic reflection until you have something to reflect upon, although reflection on prior experience from outside the present curriculum could be important very early on.

"Although your material looks interesting, we do not think that this would be something we could promote more extensively within the university here—it values Hinduism over other religions and does not address, as seen by many, some of the inherent problems with Hinduism and sustainable development, such as the caste system and rebirth." This argument has featured in two of this idea's public presentations and it is a good one. Although Samkhya is an atheistic philosophy and can be detached from any religious roots, those concepts of caste and rebirth, although not inherent to the theory, are easily superimposed from the more widely read *Bhagavata* texts. These do indeed explain caste in terms of the Gunas and they often represent Sattva as the spiritual platform from which to escape the cycle of rebirth. Of course, the origins of the Gunas lie in the ancient *Vedas*; references can be found in the early *Brhadāranyaka* and *Chandogya Upanisads* among other sources. Here, Harzer (2005) detects two layers of thought: first, the opposites of Sattva and Tamas, light versus dark, water and food, and then a later addition, the red of fire, Rajas, as suggested by the season of harvest, which resolves the tension between the two. The later 18 major *Puranic* texts, which are a sourcebook for much of modern Hinduism, are classified into three groups of six by reference to the Gunas and their presiding deities: Sattvic: Visnu (The Preserver); Rajasic: Brahma (The Creator); and Tamasic: Shiva (The Destroyer). Of course, the Gunas are an intellectual tool, a mental hammer; they may be used for many purposes.

So is this idea damned by association? I feel that there is something of a catch-22 situation here. It is impossible to adopt something from another cultural tradition without addressing the cultural baggage that comes along with the idea. Of course, one tends to be blind to the cultural baggage already embedded in one's own tradition. In any case, I think that adoption of one aspect of the curriculum from outside would not prevent the eclectic adoption of other elements from other cultures and for other purposes. In fact, it might be argued that, for a truly internationalized curriculum, this should be the case.

Ultimately, the best riposte that I have conceived for the above objection rests in the single word *Yoga*. Yoga is a complex ancient philosophy with similar Hindu and Vedic roots and it is equally deeply embedded in the *Bhagavadgita*. It is also taught at many British Community Centers to avid classes of local, non-Hindu, not-at-all Buddhist, people, who find the practices, especially the physical practices, useful for relaxation and stress mitigation. So, could not the Gunas be a Yoga for the educational curriculum? "So, what you propose is the globalization of the Guna concept?" Well, this question has never yet been asked, but it is the one that gives me the most concern. Once you scrape away layers of anxiety about the unfamiliarity of Indian philosophy, and maybe some honest xenophobia, is what is actually being proposed any more than a caricature of the original, another hamburger to add to the stereotypes of globalized culture? Of course, it could be argued that the concepts of globalization are, themselves, treated as bolt-on extras in education and their discourses less theorized than recognized (Dale and Robertson, 2003; Marginson and Rhoades, 2002). However, I think that the real answer to the question is again Yoga, and its Sattvic spiritual counterpart—Meditation; both are practices that have been globalized by the New Age Movement and that have achieved widespread popularity in the West, true, some say in "degenerate forms" (Prabhavananda and Isherwood, 1944, p. 42). Still, these Indian concepts have become embedded in popular Western society for the good reason that they serve as useful antidotes to its shallow materialism and damaging work-a-day stresses. They encourage practitioners to achieve a Sattvic condition of holistic harmony and inner strength. They encourage deep thought, introspection, and deep learning about the self and they foster a different world view that values peacefulness, serenity, and renunciation of greed for the jangling baubles used as Rajasic bait by our hyperactive society. As David Orr argues, we need a different way of thinking and a new style of education that does not reinforce the destructive ways of the present (Orr, 1994). Earlier, Tagore (1917) suggested, "The highest education is that which . . . makes our life in harmony with all existence" (p. 116). This is why, so Orr (1994) continues, that our world ". . . needs people who live well in their places . . . to make the world habitable and humane" (p. 53), i.e., more Sattvic, but less Rajasic and Tamasic. Kofi Annan (2001), our former United Nations Secretary General, once remarked, "Our biggest challenge in this new century is to take an idea that sounds abstract—sustainable development—and turn it into a reality for all the World's people" (p. 2). A Sattvic curriculum might help realize this goal.

Conclusion

The Sattvic curriculum structure has many benefits, but a key one is that it shifts the emphasis of education away from training to self-development. As geographer Yi Fu Tuan (2004, pp. 3–5) notes, "The self . . . is not fixed. We continue to discover who we are as we open ourselves . . . ." Tuan's recipe involves the challenge of coping with difficult and strange ideas, which the Sattvic curriculum may help highlight. Its structure leads the learner away from the darkness of selfish inertia, through inspiration and creative enactment, to reflection and introspection combined with a holistic vision. It leads from passive dependency through instrumental active learning to self-aware independence. It shifts the learner from consumer, through critic and creator, to conscience, conserver, and contemplative.

To sum up, currently, internationalizing the curriculum means adding multicultural elements to a Western curriculum. Here, I suggest an alternative, a whole-curriculum framework founded in the non-Western Samkhya tradition. Despite deep roots in Indian philosophy, its framework is simple. It provides a curricular superstructure with three easy stages, each with their own educational goals. Its foundation is the Gunas, the three modes of material nature, which, in different combinations, color, condition, and control everything in the material world. Sattva is everything light, sentient, serene, and peaceful; Rajas everything that is active, dynamic, and creative, and Tamas everything immobile, inert, and dark. In education, Tamas is the inertia that discourages learning and which must be overcome through inspiration and skill development. Rajas is dynamic experience, which encourages learners to focus on things in active, but instrumental terms. Sattva is contemplative and conceives the world less as a set of resources and challenges but more as an ethical and philosophical puzzle that must be resolved as a whole, not least by self-development. Sattvic learners reflect, empathize, and appreciate the unity of existence, they seek to preserve its integrity through service. In curricular terms: level 1 is about dispelling Tamas, level 2 is about engaging Rajas, and level 3 is about Sattvic harmonization and reflection. The structure provides a theoretical basis for things that many educators already try to achieve, but as a truly internationalized curriculum should, its embedded non-Western spiritual ideology might come to affect much of that conducted in its name, perhaps to the benefit of modern educational movements on citizenship and sustainability.

References

Annan, K. Secretary General calls for break in political stalemate over environmental issues, *United Nations Press Release*: SC/SM/7739 for 3/15/2001. Retrieved on April 30, 2004, from http://www.un.org/News/Press/docs/2001/sgsm7739.doc.htm

Arulmani, G. "Counselling Psychology in India: At the Confluence of Two Traditions." *Applied Psychology*, 2007, 56(1), 69–82.

Berry, T. M. *The Great Work.* New York: Belltower, 1999.

Dale, R., and Robertson, S. L. "Editorial Introduction." *Globalisation, Societies and Education*, 2003, 1(1), 3–11.

Delors, J. *Learning: The Treasure Within.* Paris: UNESCO, 1996.

Dewey, J. "Interest and Effort in Education." In J. Dewey and J. Ratner (eds.), *Intelligence in the Modern World: John Dewey's Philosophy.* New York: Random House, 1939.

Haigh, M. "Internationalization, Planetary Citizenship and Higher Education Inc." *Compare: A Journal of Comparative Education*, 2008, 38(4), 427–440.

Haigh, M. *The Sattvic Curriculum: Exploring Environmental Education for Sustainable Development.* Enfield, NH: Science Publishers, 2009.

Harzer, E. "Samkhya." In L. Jones (ed.), *Encyclopedia of Religion.* (2nd ed.) Detroit: Macmillan Reference, 2005.

Huppes, N. *Psychic Education.* New Delhi: Sri Aurobindo Education Society, 2001.

Jackson, N. J., and Shaw, M. "Subject Perspectives in Creativity." In N. J. Jackson, M. Oliver, M. Shaw, and J. Wisdom (eds.), *Developing Creativity in Higher Education: An Imaginative Curriculum.* London: Routledge-Falmer, 2006.

Johari, H. *Ayurvedic Healing Cuisines.* Rochester, VT: Healing Arts Press, 2000.

Kumarappa, J. C. *Economy of Permanence.* Kashi: Akhil Bharat Sarva-Seva-Sangh, 1945.

Larson, G. J. *Classical Samkhya.* (2nd ed.) Delhi: Motilal Banarsidass, 1979.

Marginson, S., and Rhoades, G. "Beyond National States, Markets, and Systems of Higher Education: A Glonacal Agency Heuristic." *Higher Education,* 2002, *43,* 281–309.

Milojevic, I. *Educational Futures.* London: Routledge, 2005.

Naess, A. "Self-Realization: An Ecological Approach to Being in the World." *Trumpeter,* 1987, *4,* 128–131.

Orr, D. W. *Earth in Mind.* Washington, D.C.: Island Press, 1994.

Prabhavananda, S., and Isherwood, C. *Patanjali Yoga Sutras.* Mylapore, Madras: Sri Ramakrishna Math, 1944.

Prabhupada, A. C., and Bhaktivedanta, S. *Bhagavadgita as It Is.* Los Angeles: Bhaktivedanata Book Trust, 1972.

Purkey, W. W., and Stanley, P. A. *Invitational Teaching, Learning, and Living.* Washington, D.C.: National Education Association, 1991. (ERIC Document ED340689) Retrieved on August 1, 2007, from http://www.eric.ed.gov/ERICDocs/data/ericdocs2sql/content_storage_01/0000019b/80/23/80/71.pdf

Ramakrishna Rao, K. R. "The Gunas of Prakriti According to the Samkhya Philosophy." *Philosophy East and West,* 1963, *13*(1), 61–71.

Ramakrishnananda, S. *For Thinkers on Education.* Mylapore, Madras: Sri Ramakrishna Math, 1948.

Sandal, M. L. *Siddhanta Darsanam of Vyasa.* Allahabad: B.D. Basu, 1925.

Sidhu, R. "Governing International Education in Australia." *Globalisation, Societies and Education,* 2004, *2*(1), 47–66.

Stier, J. "Taking a Critical Stance Toward Internationalization Ideologies in Higher Education." *Globalisation, Societies and Education,* 2004, *2*(1), 83–97.

Tagore, R. *Personality.* London: Macmillan, 1917.

Tagore, R. *The Religion of Man.* Rhinebeck, NY: Monkfish, 1930.

Tagore, R. *Towards Universal Man.* Bombay: Asia Books, 1961.

Tapasyananda, S. *Srimad Bhagavad Gita.* Mylapore, Madras: Sri Ramakrishna Math, 1984.

Tuan, Y. F. *Place, Art and Self.* Chicago: Columbia College, 2004.

UNESCO. *UN Decade of Education for Sustainable Development 2005–2014, International Implementation Scheme, Draft.* Paris: UNESCO, 2004. Retrieved on July 18, 2005, from http://portal.unesco.org/education/admin/ev.php?URL_ID=36026andURL_DO=DO_TOPICandURL_SECTION=201andreload=1099410445.

Vivekananda, S. *The Complete Works of Swami Vivekananda.* Calcutta: Advaita Ashrama, 1989.

Wolf, D. B. "A Psychometric Analysis of the Three Gunas." *Psychological Reports,* 1999, *84,* 1379–1390.

MARTIN HAIGH *is professor of geography at Oxford Brookes University in England and co-editor of the* Journal of Geography in Higher Education.

7

Partnering with Rotary International and residents of Xicotepec, Mexico, the University of Iowa Colleges of Engineering, Pharmacy, and Liberal Arts & Sciences have created a cross-disciplinary, international service-learning course whose impact through the years will respond to student-learning and community-identified needs.

Bridging the Distance: Service Learning in International Perspective

Jean C. Florman, Craig Just, Tomomi Naka, Jim Peterson, Hazel H. Seaba

Thanks to their partnership with a group of dedicated members of Rotary International District 6000 (eastern Iowa), people in a town in east-central Mexico are drinking cleaner water and their children are benefiting from improved dental and health care, a refurbished elementary school with a new library, and new secondary school classrooms. The impact of this long-term partnership has been keenly felt by Iowans as well as the residents of Xicotepec, where both the elementary school and a local street now bear the name "Rotario." When eastern Iowa Rotarians began to discuss plans for an international humanitarian project in 2001, they hoped to incorporate a service-learning element to their relationship with Xicotepec. They could not anticipate, however, that their idea also would grow into a major service-learning course involving faculty, staff, and students from three University of Iowa colleges, with commitments from the University to nurture the course and the international partnerships for the long-term.

Background

The Xicotepec Project began in 2002, when Iowa City resident Gary Pacha created a centerpiece project for his 2002–2003 tenure as District Governor of Rotary District 6000. Gary, his wife Nancy, who is a former high-school Spanish teacher, and Ray Muston, former District 6000 Governor and University of Iowa associate professor emeritus, brought together Rotarians

NEW DIRECTIONS FOR TEACHING AND LEARNING, no. 118, Summer 2009 © Wiley Periodicals, Inc.
Published online in Wiley InterScience (www.interscience.wiley.com) • DOI: 10.1002/tl.354

and young people from the United States and Mexico to help address community-identified needs in the town of Xicotepec, which boasts a small but active Rotary Club.

From the beginning, the project united complementary assets: the experience and resources of Rotarians coupled with the energy and idealism of youth. It offered eastern Iowa high school and university students a unique opportunity to provide service in an international setting, gain the deep personal satisfaction that comes from performing service work, and forge permanent international friendships. As educators, Ray and Nancy also were convinced that the learning opportunities embodied in an international service project could be life-changing and adaptable in an academically meaningful way to a broad range of disciplines. They hoped University of Iowa faculty members would eventually go beyond encouraging their students to volunteer in Xicotepec to create systematic, course-based learning opportunities. Through a happy coincidence of events and people, this dream was fulfilled in spring semester 2007.

Five years earlier, however, Iowa City businessman Jim Peterson launched the Xicotepec/Iowa partnership by leading a team of six fellow Rotarians on a weeklong "Discovery Trip" to Xicotepec to investigate possible collaborations between the two communities. In February 2002, the group refined the project goals to include:

- Hands-on, humanitarian service
- Attention to the self-identified needs of Xicotepec
- Strong, long-term relationships between partner clubs
- Development as a model for other projects
- The development of a service-learning component for University of Iowa students

Based on the needs expressed by the Xicotepec residents in early 2002 and the Xicotepec club's pledge to partner with the Iowa Rotarians, District 6000 decided to provide four new classrooms for one of the Mexican community's primary schools. The commitment by the Iowa service group included both sweat equity and $25,000 for construction materials. Within two hours of a fifteen-minute presentation unveiling the project, group members had pledged the entire amount.

During the next five years, Iowa Rotarians and their Xicotepec counterparts launched a series of needs analyses focusing on education, public safety, healthcare delivery, and water quality, and project teams collaborated to begin addressing community needs. Since the inception of the project, more than 240 people have made close to 350 visits to the Mexican community, and monetary and in-kind donations from Rotary International, individuals, and Iowa universities have been worth hundreds of thousands of dollars. Using their own personal funds, several Rotarians travel throughout the year to help sustain this active partnership with Xicotepec residents.

NEW DIRECTIONS FOR TEACHING AND LEARNING • DOI: 10.1002/tl

In addition, teams of as many as 50 individuals—roughly half of whom are high school, University of Iowa, and Iowa State University students—spend one or two weeks at a time in the town during spring break or the summer to work on ongoing projects.

Since January 2004 when District 6000 Rotarians shipped a fire truck and a school bus to the town, Project Teams have built four new classrooms at the primary school, established scholarship funds for students too poor to attend school, created a beautiful, well-stocked school library, screened more than 200 women each year for cervical cancer, identified the secondary school as a priority project, provided health screening and dental education to hundreds of local children, and launched an impressive series of events and projects focusing on drinking water and sanitation. In the process, long-term relationships have been established with several organizations in Xicotepec, including the local Red Cross and orphanage. In recognition of the success of this major, long-term international partnership, Iowa Campus Compact—an organization of college and university presidents that support and encourage volunteerism and service-learning—named Rotary International District 6000 a 2006 Iowa Campus Compact Community Partnership Award honoree.

One of Rotary's fundamental goals is to increase world peace and understanding. Through the Xicotepec project, "internationalization" has taken place in both directions: visitors from the United States have gained a better understanding and greater appreciation for Mexico and its citizens, and the people of Xicotepec have come to see Norte Americanos in a different light. In a documentary made by former Iowa City High School student Anita Rao—a frequent participant in the project—Xicotepec resident Jaime Wurts says, "People here no longer call them 'gringo.' Instead, they are our brothers and sisters from the U.S."

The two-way street between the two communities also has been enhanced by the Rotary Youth Exchange, which arranged for four high school students from both countries to be exchange students in Xicotepec and Iowa. Several Mexican college students have come to Iowa City to work in internship programs. Unfortunately, the universities and technical school in the Xicotepec area are not a perfect "fit" with the University of Iowa, which is a large, research-intensive school. Prior to the spring 2008 visit, however, two University of Iowa faculty members (Professor of Pharmacy Hazel Seaba and Associate Research Engineer Craig Just) and Iowa Rotarian Jim Peterson invited faculty and students from Benemérita Universidad Autónoma de Puebla (BUAP) to participate in the de-worming and water treatment projects and to discuss the potential for developing a more intense, ongoing relationship between the two schools.

From the beginning, the relationship between the Iowa and Mexican communities has been truly collaborative, with Xicotepec residents fully invested in determining local needs, developing possible solutions, constructing buildings, raising funds, and traveling to Iowa. During the first year, the Xicotepec Rotary Club raised $7,000 (U.S.), an enormous sum, given the size of the club (18 members) and the community's limited resources. Xicotepec community members also feed, lodge, and provide local transportation to their partners from the United States.

The support from the local Xicotepec community is significant and growing. The small local Rotary Club of 18 men, an equivalent number of women in the affiliated women's service club, Inner Wheel, and the District Governor of Rotary District 4180 have been critical to planning and facilitating visits since the earliest years of the project. Local government leaders, including the mayor, city council members, and municipal officials of the water and sewer utility and municipal medical staff help facilitate approvals and provide staff support. Teachers, staff members, and parents' groups at the local schools, the Xicotepec chapter of the Red Cross, and the Catholic Church contribute sweat equity, resources, and facilities—including the convent where many of the U.S. students stay. Dr. Jorge Octavio Martinez offers his obstetrics/gynecology and organizational skills at the annual Just-in-Time Cervical Cancer Screening Project, sponsored by Rotary District 4180. Xicotepec Project participants from the United States volunteer during the annual clinic as well as at the local orphanage, Casa Hogar Victoria.

When project members from the U.S. are in town, local media report on their activities and many local merchants welcome the Iowans' presence, as a spike occurs in the sale of plumbing supplies, building materials, hardware, computer supplies, phone cards, bottled water, Internet café time, and straw hats.

Engineering Students and Faculty Involvement

In an effort to include even more volunteers and broaden the scope of expertise, District 6000 Rotarians have involved university students and faculty in the Xicotepec Project. Engineering students at the University of Iowa and Iowa State University have volunteered countless hours to help Xicotepec sanitation workers and Rotarians design and build systems to improve drinking water, sanitation, and environmental quality. Relying on their own resources and support from District 6000, University of Iowa students in Engineers for a Sustainable World (ESW) and their faculty sponsor, Associate Research Engineer (civil and environmental engineering) Craig Just, have traveled to Xicotepec every Spring Break since 2003. ESW members work to fight poverty, provide access to safe drinking water, and promote sustainable social and economic communities around the world.

After several years, however, Craig decided to maximize student learning by transforming the Xicotepec volunteer experience into a formal, service-learning course in civil and environmental engineering. In May 2006, he was accepted into the University of Iowa's weeklong Service Learning Institute, sponsored by the Center for Teaching and conducted by Edward Zlotkowski, Professor of English at Bentley College (MA) and Campus Compact Senior Faculty Fellow.

NEW DIRECTIONS FOR TEACHING AND LEARNING • DOI: 10.1002/tl

Funded by the Office of the Provost, the two Service Learning Institutes, in May 2005 and 2006, provided training and resources in service-learning pedagogy and a small stipend to 30 faculty participants from every UI college but one. Although only required to create one new service-learning course apiece, the institute members actually created forty-nine. More than 1,250 students participated in the courses during the first two years of the three-year cycle, and as of May 2007, they have contributed more than 28,000 hours of service in the state of Iowa and Xicotepec. Following the institute, faculty members also participated in a variety of additional events and activities, including assessment of student learning in the new service-learning courses and a public showcase of the courses in October 2007.

As institute members began outlining the service-learning courses they planned to design, Craig's commitment to Xicotepec caught the interest of two other institute members, Assistant Dean of Pharmacy Hazel Seaba and Assistant Professor of Journalism Lyombe (Leo) Eko. The three Institute members decided to collaborate to create a cross-disciplinary service-learning course during which students would learn, travel, and work together as part of the Rotary District 6000 Xicotepec Project.

Course Design for "International Perspectives: Xicotepec"

Servicing learning is a way of teaching and learning that incorporates community engagement into academic coursework (see www.compact.org; www.centeach.uiowa.edu). Although a challenge, transforming what was originally a volunteer activity by engineering students and their instructor into a full-fledged service-learning course for engineering, pharmacy, and journalism students proved to be a resounding success.

The multidisciplinary course was designed to introduce students to the benefits, challenges, and logistics of partnering with nonprofit institutions and community members to provide service in a community in a less developed country. In collaboration with Rotary International and local community members, students developed discipline-specific projects aimed at identifying and addressing community needs (particularly healthcare, social service, and environmental quality) in Xicotepec. As in any service-learning course, the instructors expected students to use both critical thinking skills and guided reflection to enhance their disciplinary knowledge and skills as well as to enrich the experiences they gained through meaningful service in Xicotepec.

Before the end of the weeklong 2006 Service Learning Institute, Craig, Hazel, Leo, Center for Teaching Associate Director Jean Florman, and Rotarian Jim Peterson (with input from Gary and Nancy Pacha, Ray Muston, and several other Rotarians) met to begin hammering out details about course content, learning requirements, project design, travel, and funding. Tomomi Naka, a Ph.D. candidate in anthropology and a graduate assistant at the

Center for Teaching, was appointed to the teaching assistant position for the course.

Because of his central importance as a Xicotepec Project leader, Jim Peterson served as an instructor-of-record in the service-learning course. Without Jim's logistical legerdemain, the course likely would have taken years to develop. Fluent in Spanish, he arranged plane reservations, housing, and meals (instructors in homes; students in a local convent) for some 50 Iowa participants, including university faculty members and students, high school students, and Iowa Rotarians. He also served as the interface between the Xicotepec community and the service-learning students and faculty, helping to set up projects and responding to unexpected situations in Mexico.

Shortly before the semester began, Leo was forced to bow out as an instructor. As luck would have it, Center for Teaching Associate Director Jean Florman is a professional writer and has taught upper-division undergraduate writing courses at the University of Iowa; she stepped in to teach the students who enrolled in "International Perspectives" as a writing course.

The model partnership already developed by the Rotary proved to be the foundation for success for development of the service-learning course. For example, one of the fundamental principles of service learning is that community organizations and individuals must be full partners in any effort to identify and address community need. From the beginning of the Xicotepec Project, members of Rotary District 6000 committed themselves to a similar model of full partnership and shared responsibility for identifying and addressing community needs. This has never been a relationship of noblesse oblige or of gringo "experts" identifying another community's problems and then coming in to "solve" them with culturally inappropriate techniques and resources.

Reflecting the disciplines of the instructors, "International Perspectives: Xicotepec" was listed for credit in Civil and Environmental Engineering, Pharmacy, and Journalism. The instructors chose the course number "126" as a tribute to a local restaurant of the same name where a number of course planning sessions as well as Service Learning Institute meetings had taken place.

The instructors designed the nine-week course to include seven weeks of coursework and project design prior to the spring break trip to Xicotepec, a week performing service in Xicotepec, and then one week in Iowa City during which students prepared public presentations about their service efforts and the knowledge and skills acquired during the course. During the course, the four instructors, sixteen undergraduate or professional ("Pharm D") students, and one graduate student met weekly for two hours. The first hour of each class was devoted to presentations and discussion of topics of interest (or concern) to all the students: cultural competence, the culture and history of Xicotepec, the nature of the Rotary project, and guided reflection exercises to link community service to content learning.

The instructors also tried to anticipate and address a variety of logistical issues presented by the course, including questions about visas and passports, immunizations and travel health, and housing, food, and language abilities. A guest lecturer also talked about teamwork and team building.

The second hour of each class was devoted to "break-out" sessions during which the engineering, pharmacy, and writing teams separated to focus on the content and skills specifically related to their disciplines.

The Water Team. Course outcomes for the Water Team members—including students in engineering, urban and regional planning, and public health—included the design and installation of drinking water systems for a primary school and the Red Cross clinic in Xicotepec. To help insure the project's success, the team chose three focus areas: community engagement, technical expertise, and university/professional engagement.

The water team emphasized the use of community engagement as a design resource by generating valuable input from Xicotepec community members, facilitating discussions with local officials, and exploiting the social and technical expertise of Rotarians and other community leaders of Xicotepec. The community engagement focus also meant students utilized resources that had been identified and documented by previous UI Engineer for a Sustainable World (UI ESW) Xicotepec Project teams. Engineers can provide special expertise to developing communities in a number of areas, including water, sanitation, energy, and food security. The Water Team understood that however things might appear to them, lack of accessibility to safe drinking water would only truly be a problem if identified as such by the community itself. Through several years of engagement in Xicotepec, previous UI ESW teams had learned from neighborhood leaders and residents that they indeed wanted better access to safe drinking water.

Part of the work yet to be done in this course is the development of a performance matrix by which "success" or "failure"—again, as viewed by the community members themselves—can be measured. Such a performance matrix would go beyond mere technical evaluation to provide a more complete picture of successes and shortcomings of projects.

To make a real contribution to developing communities, engineers must provide technical expertise—solutions to problems that would not or could not be provided by other, equally talented professionals from other disciplines. Engineers need to be trained to think "out of the box" or "critically," and then to utilize available resources to obtain meaningful outcomes. Unfortunately, engineers from the developed world often see the only useful resources as computers, steel, concrete, chemicals, technology, etc., while ignoring resources such as people, culture, natural capital, and history. Students learned that advanced technologies and methods that work well in a wealthy society may be inappropriate for use in a poorer country. For example, the engineer accustomed to an environment of high labor costs and abundant financial capital may correctly decide to employ specialized tools, machinery, and technologies, thereby reducing the need for human labor. However, in a country where unemployment is a problem, cheap labor is abundant and capital is very expensive—economic and social considerations may lead the engineer to a different solution.

Students in the Xicotepec course also learned that community resources that are constructed, purchased, or implemented with outside support—such as that provided by the Water Team—must be operated and maintained long after the outside partner has gone. In the past, the unmet need for expertise within the community to operate and maintain such a resource has often limited its long-term sustainability and severely curtailed the benefits derived by the community compared to what they might have been otherwise. Because students from the University of Iowa are inherently temporary visitors to the community and because drinking water purification systems require some technical expertise to install, operate, and maintain, the drinking water systems in Xicotepec were designed and installed in partnership with local professionals, tradesmen, and laborers as well as local university students and staff to create the necessary expertise within the community to properly operate and maintain the systems, which, in turn, insures that the community derives their full benefits.

The focus on university/professional engagement led to meetings and seminars that provided technology and cultural transfer to Xicotepec students, professors, professionals, tradesmen and laborers. The support of Mexican community leaders was critical because without it, an otherwise technically sound project might fail. Even with the best preparation, outside technical teams may not be able to effectively communicate the basic intention and future maintenance or operational needs of a project without the collaboration, intervention, or mediation of locals and professionals, specialists and educators.

The Pharmacy Team. Pharmacists who understand the needs of diverse patients and populations can improve healthcare access to patients and their communities. Global health experiences provide a reference that allow us to better understand our own health care environment and public health policy. In our global, highly mobile society, the lack of health of any individual can affect widely dispersed geographic populations; the health of each individual is relevant to the health of all. These concepts are well developed in "Why Global Health Matters," RX for Survival, http://www.pbs.org/wgbh/rxforsurvival/series/atters/index.html.

The next generation of pharmacists will practice in a world that expects the profession to be patient-oriented and also to contribute to the health of the public at large (population-based care). Patient-oriented care and population-based care each have a local and a global face, and underpinning each is a professional obligation to foster social justice. The knowledge and skills of tomorrow's pharmacists must benefit equally all segments of our population, both local and global. Communities around the world face a critical need for adequate access to health care and essential medications. To meet these complex pharmacy and healthcare challenges, students need both coursework and experience in the context of underserved populations and global health.

In 2006, the University of Iowa College of Pharmacy offered senior Pharm D students several advanced pharmacy practice experiences (APPEs), including experience with pharmacy practice to underserved populations. No experiences in international settings were available, however. To determine the suitability of the Xicotepec project for a service-learning course, Assistant Dean of Pharmacy Hazel Seaba participated in the 2006 trip to Xicotepec with the goal of identifying projects that would require knowledge of medication management coupled with an opportunity to provide medication management to an underserved population.

Xicotepec Rotarians had previously identified deworming for preschool and elementary school children as a medication management project that would be highly valued in the community. Intestinal worms are estimated to infect 27 percent of the children in this community, and even more in the town's poorest areas. Deworming in schools is an important public health activity and is considered safe and effective by the World Health Organization (World Bank, March 2003).

This project presented classic, content-rich medication management challenges for the students, such as: What is the drug of choice? What dose is appropriate? What dosage form is most effective? Where can the product be purchased at the best price? How can the product be transported to Xicotepec? What is the best administration procedure? and, How can medication administration records be properly recorded?

In addition to the deworming project, Pharm D students also administered tooth fluoridation to more than 2,000 elementary school children in the community. One of their pre-trip assignments required them to also research and write an informational brochure to inform their peers about possible travel healthcare concerns and appropriate medications.

The overall goal for the Pharm D students was to prepare them to successfully function in a profession-specific manner in a less-developed country. In partnership with Rotary International and members of the Xicotepec community, Hazel and the pharmacy students planned and executed a pharmaceutical management service project. Through the course and the experiences in Xicotepec, the students developed their role as pharmacists practicing in international health service. The course also enhanced the students' knowledge and understanding of their primary discipline as well as their personal and professional growth.

The "Write" Team. Students on the "Write Team" read and wrote several genres of nonfiction writing, including newspaper articles, feature pieces, and personal essays. They also explored ethical issues in journalism and the role of the participant-observer. In addition, like the other teams, the writers were required to produce some form of reflective writing in response to questions designed to link their content and skills learning to their experiential learning.

In addition to completing a series of brief writing assignments through-out the course, Write Team members also were responsible for writing a fea-ture article about their service efforts in Xicotepec, producing a written product of use to the local community, and keeping a reflection journal. The written products included a project proposal for a retirement home, an advertising poster and an explanatory brochure about a women's health clinic (both in Spanish), and four articles about the service-learning course for publication in a Spanish-language newspaper. Student reflections were sparked by specific questions that Jean posed about their learning goals for the course, self-assessments of their learning styles, and observations and reflections of their experiences during the week in Xicotepec.

As the course continued, both anticipation and anxiety increased for the Write Team students. One of their main concerns involved lack of flu-ency in Spanish. In addition, unlike the other two teams, the writing team had no specific projects awaiting them in Xicotepec. Because Craig had been taking engineering students to Xicotepec for five years, he not only knew the community well, but also was involved in ongoing engineering projects related to water delivery services. During winter break 2006, Hazel had accompanied Jim and other Rotarians to the town where she learned from local residents about their healthcare needs and possible projects for her students. In contrast, the writing students were not linked to any par-ticular community effort, and, in fact, were uncertain about what commu-nity needs their journalistic skills might help address. This group of students did not even share a disciplinary focus—their majors included journalism, women's studies, management and organizations, and psychol-ogy, and except for the journalism student, they had never written for a "public" nonacademic audience. Their anxiety was heightened by the fact that their instructor (Jean) was the only member of the teaching team who was not traveling to Xicotepec.

In an effort to help them understand the nature of service-learning courses, Jean assigned readings and guided discussion around the issue of how students might design and direct their own service-learning experi-ences. The students were intrigued, but it was clear that they felt more angst in comparison to members of the other two teams, which had specific proj-ects awaiting them. Fortunately, Jim Peterson and teaching assistant Tomomi Naka provided critical support to the writing team members. Before the spring break trip, Jim described several community issues that Xicote-pec residents had discussed in the past: the need for living space for the elderly; the economic potential of an outdoor market for artisans; and the importance of disseminating information about women's healthcare dur-ing an annual clinic that would take place the week the students visited. Both Jim and Tomomi also helped the writing team during the week in Mex-ico, when the students needed to connect with local residents or be in con-tact with members of the Iowa contingent. To their credit, the writing team members rose to the challenge, and not only "found" their own projects and community partners, but also reflected favorably on the value of taking control of their own learning experiences and forging partnerships with community members.

Funding

Travel to Mexico and a week's stay in Xicotepec cost $1,000 per person. Reflecting the Rotary's spirit of volunteerism and meaningful service, the course required students to provide $200 from their own resources. The instructors felt that this figure would not be prohibitive for UI students, as they could earn and save small amounts during the weeks leading up to the trip. By requiring students to use personal resources, the instructors felt they were reinforcing the message that although fun and fulfilling, this was not going to be an all-expenses-paid spring break blowout, but rather a serious endeavor that required a significant commitment on their part.

Iowa City Rotarians provided matching grants to help defray the cost of the trip, and additional support was provided by the University's Study Abroad Office, Center for Teaching, Colleges of Engineering and Pharmacy, and Student Government. Pharmacy students held a pancake breakfast and made personal appeals, which netted $1,200. The funds provided additional medication support to the Xicotepec clinics conducted during the trip.

Instructors paid their own way. The Center for Teaching provided funding for teaching assistant Tomomi Naka.

Learning from Experience

Despite the considerable success of this course, the project was not without challenges. Even before leaving Iowa, several international students had to jump through a number of extra administrative hoops to enable them to travel to Mexico and be re-admitted to the United States. One student had to drive five hours (each way) for a five-minute meeting with the Mexican consular official in Omaha. A Canadian student who had applied but not yet received a green card had to drop the course because international travel would have been impossible.

In the past, project team members had little trouble bringing boxes of supplies into Mexico as personal carry-on luggage. During the 2007 service-learning course, however, airport security personnel would not allow 37 boxes of donated items and project supplies to enter the country without prior approval and detailed manifests. The boxes contained donations of healthcare products such as baby care products and toys. More critically, they also contained items critical to the service-learning projects. Despite repeated requests from project leader Jim Peterson, the supplies were held in Mexico City and never released during the time the Iowa teams were in the country.

"International Perspectives" students and faculty members brainstormed and scrambled for solutions—transforming a serious roadblock into another learning experience. The boxes contained fluoride solutions that students planned to "paint" onto the teeth of elementary school children. When the boxes were waylaid, the Pharm D students—with the help of Jim and Hazel—secured disposable fluoride trays that proved to be much more efficient—if more expensive.

Other course content and pedagogy issues also developed—not surprising, given the variety of disciplines represented by instructors and students. Although the writing students relished the reflection exercises, for instance, pharmacy students were not as familiar or comfortable with this self-analytic style of writing.

By the end of the course, students and faculty members agreed that future Xicotepec courses should be designed for a full semester; in fact, the students requested an additional week after they returned to better prepare for their public presentations.

In addition, participants felt that students needed additional in-depth information about the history, culture, and economy of the community. A broader socio-economic and historic context would greatly enrich the students' experiences. For instance, engineering students may design and build a very functional water treatment system, but they also should be attuned to potential cultural and economic issues. What will happen, for example, if the filters are not easily available from a distant supplier? Or the man who is supposed to take care of the system has to leave town to find work elsewhere? These are the kinds of questions that students can explore if they have previously learned more about the community and its history.

And there are always variables beyond organizers' control. In 2008, for example, Holy Week celebrations in Mexico coincided with spring break at the University of Iowa. Like other Mexican communities, Xicotepec virtually shuts down as local residents celebrate and worship, so University of Iowa students did not spend their 2008 spring break in Xicotepec. Yet viewed from the right perspective, problems can become learning experiences. The course instructors planned around Holy Week, and in 2008, students had the option of traveling the week after spring break, following semester's end, or during the summer. Though Pharm D students in their second and third years were not able to participate in spring 2008, fourth-year students could enroll and travel to Xicotepec in an elective clinical rotation. And in the future, the course will be longer and course content redesigned to meet the explicit learning goals of students.

From the beginning, "International Perspectives: Xicotepec" (and the Xicotepec Project itself) has been grounded in the belief that service must be a collaborative, long-term effort. When Iowa Rotarians returned to Xicotepec in 2003, one of the Mexican club members told them, "When you left last year, we did not think you would be back." That skepticism is not uncommon in communities that have seen Americans descend on them to declare community needs, "do good deeds," and then disappear. Through the Xicotepec Project, Iowa Rotarians, university students, faculty, and staff members have shattered this image for people in Xicotepec. Designed from the beginning to be an ongoing partnership, the service-learning course has grown into a multifaceted endeavor that has changed the lives of everyone involved.

More particularly, the course has internationalized the curriculum at the University of Iowa in a unique way. Although a number of UI undergraduate, graduate, and professional school courses offer study abroad experience, International Perspectives is Iowa's only international *service-learning* course. This means the Xicotepec volunteer experience—including preparation and follow-up as well as the spring break trip—is a fundamentally *academic* experience. Collaborative community service is analogous to a course textbook in that both can teach course content, be it civil engineering, pharmacy, or writing. As with any service-learning course, students learn about the people with whom they volunteer (and vice versa). But the *international* aspect of this course means students are pushed to learn about people who are considerably different from themselves. The course—and the Rotary partners in particular—push students to open their minds, take risks, and test their skills, flexibility, determination, and character.

In addition to learning about another culture, students also examine environmental, healthcare, and educational problems in a *global and cross-cultural* context while also partnering with community members to develop practical, long-term solutions appropriate to the town's *local* social, economic, and historical contexts.

The "internationalizing" impact of this course continues to be felt on the University of Iowa campus as well as in Xicotepec. One Iowa student enrolled in another course during which she traveled to India where she studied women's health issues in community contexts. The Xicotepec experience inspired another student to seek a graduate degree in public health with a special emphasis on non-U.S. populations. In March 2008, a third student returned to Xicotepec with Hazel Seaba, Craig Just, and Jim Peterson to continue project efforts and plan for the 2009 course.

And as the impact of this experience continues to spin outward as students look back on their experiences, the course itself continues to morph into a newer, richer opportunity for students, faculty members, Rotarians, and the Xicotepec community. The full-semester spring 2009 iteration of "International Perspectives: Xicotepec" included two additional faculty and students from Spanish as a field of study and the College of Education. In addition, the inaugural course faculty decided to test their technological mettle and will require future students to report and reflect on their experiences through a special Xicotepec blog site. In addition to weekly interaction during the U.S.-component of the course, students will be expected to blog while in Xicotepec.

And, as always, our Xicotepec partners will be encouraged to join in the conversation so that we might better understand.

Reference

World Bank. "School Deworming at a Glance." Washington, D.C.: World Bank, March 2003.

JEAN C. FLORMAN is the associate director of the University of Iowa Center for Teaching. Her background is in anthropology and law, and before joining the Center, she worked as a writer and public radio producer.

CRAIG JUST is an associate research engineer at IIHR – Hydroscience & Engineering at the University of Iowa. He teaches and researches global issues related to water, watershed processes, environmental contaminants, and human health relevant to rich and poor countries.

TOMOMI NAKA is a graduate assistant at the Center for Teaching and a Ph.D. candidate in the Anthropology Department of the University of Iowa. She is researching economic decision making in a Pennsylvania Mennonite community.

JIM PETERSON has worked for twenty-five years in the telecommunications industry with positions in the United States, Africa, Europe, Latin America, and the Caribbean. As a Rotarian, he has coordinated the Xicotepec Project full time since 2002.

HAZEL H. SEABA is a professor and assistant dean for assessment and curriculum in the College of Pharmacy at the University of Iowa where she teaches in the areas of drug information and medication management for underserved populations.

NEW DIRECTIONS FOR TEACHING AND LEARNING • DOI: 10.1002/tl

8

Colleagues from Virginia Tech and Mzuzu University personnel worked together to redesign an online master's degree program to fit Malawi's needs.

Context-Oriented Instructional Design for Course Transformation

Ross A. Perkins

Instructional designers working in international settings are often interested in reports on how particular courses or programs have been implemented in other contexts; doing so either confirms or extends their own experiences. In the hope that such information can benefit the larger design community, this chapter specifically shows how contextual elements have impacted instructional design decisions. The chapter begins with an overview of a specific project that sought to create Web-based classes for learners in Malawi. It continues by relating formative evaluation data collected through feedback of selected courses that were pilot tested. The conclusion of the chapter focuses on implications for course developers regarding context-based design, and a few thoughts on internationalization and design.

Overview of the Project

The United States Agency for International Development (USAID) developed a program known as the University Partnerships for Institutional Capacity (UPIC) in late 2000, asking for proposals that followed three lines of capacity building: administrative leadership development, teacher education, and instructional technology. Faculty in the Department of Teaching and Learning at Virginia Polytechnic Institute and State University (Virginia Tech) were awarded two of the three grants in 2001. The first

NEW DIRECTIONS FOR TEACHING AND LEARNING, no. 118, Summer 2009 © Wiley Periodicals, Inc.
Published online in Wiley InterScience (www.interscience.wiley.com) • DOI: 10.1002/tl.355

would focus on the training of bachelor's degree holders who would earn a master's degree and then serve as a core faculty for a newly created bachelor's degree program for primary educators. The second grant, the focus of this article, was known by the acronym ICET (Information Communication & Educational Technology). Both grants paired Virginia Tech with two different institutions of higher education in Malawi, Africa, and established an initial five-year relationship, though contacts between the institutions continue. The objective of the UPIC-ICET initiative was to train a cadre from the partner institution (Mzuzu University, or MZUNI) who would function as the instructional designers and distance program coordinators in their own institution.

Between the two USAID projects awarded to Virginia Tech (one for primary education, and the UPIC-ICET project), there were a total of six doctoral students and close to 30 students enrolled in two master's degree programs (approximately twenty-four in the M.A. in elementary education and six in the instructional technology M.A. Ed. program). The doctoral students from the primary education initiative, and six students from the UPIC-ICET program, came to Virginia Tech (Blacksburg, Virginia) for two years of study. The remaining master's students took courses delivered to them in Malawi by professors from Virginia Tech over a period of three years. The decision to have the doctoral students at the university for the first part of their studies was based on a residency requirement, but it was also a logistical decision, as studying in their own country would not have allowed the access to resources, the possible distraction of their job duties, and so on. They returned to complete their data collection and final writing in Malawi, with occasional face-to-face support from their U.S.-based professors. The rationale for bringing the students from Malawi to the United States was primarily based on grant funding: the UPIC-ICET project budget was nearly $1 million less than each of the other two UPIC activities. Furthermore, one of the project goals was to expose students to a large-scale implementation of information and communication technologies (ICT) at the university, which included its library system. Fees, books, and supplies were covered for all students by the grant funds. Those who traveled to the United States were provided with graduate assistantships, which helped them pay living expenses. Following the conclusion of the grant, two students who graduated under the auspices of the UPIC-ICET grant returned on their own volition (with no outside funding) to pursue doctoral studies in ICT at Virginia Tech; both were awarded assistantships by the university, and have since received scholarships.

The six lecturers from MZUNI matriculated in Virginia Tech's master's degree program in instructional technology. During their studies in the United States, the cohort would return to Malawi for a period of three months to conduct a nationwide needs assessment. The plan was created by the Malawian participants and their professors. The resulting data from the assessment are primarily what guided the course redesign over a period of two years. Following the completion of their master's degree program, which concluded in December 2003, the cohort returned to Malawi to start building the distance education program at Mzuzu (MUDEP). Within months of their return, the cadre had finalized five graduate-level courses for pilot testing. The pilot courses included Introduction to Instructional Technology, Principles of Instructional Design, Digital Media for Education, Advanced Educational Psychology, and Introduction to Educational Research. During the development phase, Virginia Tech faculty worked in person with the MUDEP faculty, but the pilot test and later implementation of the program was carried out by the Mzuzu cadre themselves.

The UPIC-ICET project itself came to a conclusion in January 2007. In the final analysis, the overall programmatic goals were successful, but the MUDEP program itself has faced difficulties with sustainability. The cohort sadly lost one member at the very start of the project—his technical expertise as the sixth member was sorely missed. Five people earned their master's degree in instructional design and technology (IDT), and all returned to provide leadership and guidance for the new MUDEP program. The team was reduced to three active members when two of the M.A. Ed. graduates returned to Virginia Tech to pursue doctoral studies in IDT. The difficulties in implementation, however, lie outside any design efforts related to the courses themselves. The remainder of this chapter, then, examines the context as established by the data from the needs assessment, the results of the evaluation of two selected pilot courses (educational psychology and educational research), and explores a context-based approach to design.

Contextual Influences on Design

Attempts to design, or in this case redesign, courses or programs for a setting different from the originally intended must be guided by a thoughtful analysis of both context and needs. One definition of context is "a multi-level body of factors in which learning and performance are embedded" (Tessmer and Richey, 1997, p. 87). A context is made up of many levels, and designers can get a sense of it through a context or environmental analysis (Dean, 1990; Tiene and Futagami, 1987; Tessmer, 1990; Tessmer and Harris, 1992).

Such an analysis is an examination of "physical and psychosocial factors that affect learning . . . a phenomenological approach to instructional design in that it seeks to describe the learning 'as it is' in the real world . . ." (Tessmer and Harris, 1992, p. 15). The implication is that the emphasis is less on what learners need to know, and focuses instead on whatever may affect, sustain, or diminish the educational process. The goal of the analysis is "to describe where an instructional product will be used, how it will be used, and how it will be sustained" (Tessmer, 1990). The foundational assumption behind the rationale of a context analysis is that it will improve the instructional design (ID) product (Tessmer and Harris, 1992).

Establishing the Context

Malawi, like many developing countries around the world, faces critical teacher shortages. Factors such as a high rate of HIV/AIDS, attrition through emigration of educated people ("brain drain"), the prevalence of virulent diseases, and the generally low status and well-known low pay of educators all contribute to a very small core of teaching professionals. The system of teacher education in the country, which again mirrors that found in many similar institutions of the global South, has a very limited capacity to train primary and secondary teachers. The fact is that even if the existing institutions were to expand their enrollment, even doubling it, there are not enough physical spaces currently built to house and teach students, and there is nowhere near the number of master's degree and doctoral degree holders to form competent faculties. Thus, if one were to rely on traditional forms of education, the ability to meet the estimated shortage of 15,000 teachers will never be met. The USAID-funded project sought to expand human capacity to help begin to build a foundation for the future of education in Malawi. With the UPIC-ICET project, the goal was to use ICT and an existing instructional design master's degree program (ITMA) to help overcome the challenges of face-to-face instruction. The proposal suggested that by training a cohort of people and giving them a graduate-level education in instructional technology, a branching effect would ensue: those trained would pass on their knowledge to larger groups, and then those groups would take it beyond. Ultimately, there would be a solid core of ICT professionals in Malawi who, with distance education, could help bridge the ever-expanding "digital divide," and help meet the personnel needs of the Ministry of Education.

As positive and forward thinking as the UPIC-ICET proposal was, and as enthusiastic Malawian and USAID officials were about it, the project personnel had yet to do a needs assessment to determine how it could actually be implemented. Early in their master's degree program, the cohort from Mzuzu would return to Malawi to conduct a nationwide needs assessment, surveying close to 200 people, most of whom were teachers, across Malawi's three districts. The report created by the team showed a number of areas that would pose challenges, with many factors directly impacting instructional design decisions. The study team reached the following conclusions.

- Forty-four percent of secondary school teachers did not have a certification that would qualify them to teach in secondary schools.
- Income levels of teachers were generally very low; hence, the amount they could spend for classes would be very low.
- Most teachers (85 percent) preferred the print mode of instructional delivery to technological modes.
- Priority for distance education programs would have to be given to addressing the needs of those teachers who are not qualified to teach at secondary schools.

NEW DIRECTIONS FOR TEACHING AND LEARNING • DOI: 10.1002/tl

• The cheapest and most convenient mode of communication in Malawi is postal service. If enough funds were available, the Internet would be a valuable mode of delivery of instruction by distance especially in urban areas.

Revising the Courses. Based on these conclusions, given the policies and capacity of Mzuzu, and the realities of the ICT infrastructure in Malawi, a number of guidelines for course and program development were put in place. First, the delivery of the program, at least initially, would be print-based, not electronic given infrastructure and access issues. The initial courses would be designed for teachers who had bachelor's degrees. The future program would focus on untrained or unqualified teachers. Another important consideration was that the program itself could not be a master's program, as doctoral-level personnel would be needed to teach it. Instead, it would be a postgraduate diploma program and offer courses that could count toward a master's degree. Finally, as courses were redesigned in the United States, the Mzuzu team would use other Malawian colleagues for formative evaluation purposes. Their feedback would help ensure that culturally relevant examples and modifications were in place, as well as to help ensure that the content was lucid.

Designers examined the following areas as courses were redesigned.

1. The language of accompanying materials (textbooks cannot be edited)—to ensure that it follows British English spellings.
2. Examples in the guidebooks—to ensure they are relevant to Malawi (includes metric conversions where necessary).
3. Representation of genders in examples—to ensure fairness and equality.
4. Materials previously delivered via the Web (such as animated graphics or Flash-based quizzes)—making sure there was a print-based format.
5. Learner assessment—to be configured in such a way that grading or feedback could be delivered via post rather than electronically.
6. Pedagogical assumptions—to see if the assumptions would need further explanation.

Pilot Testing the Modules. The instructional designers at MZUNI initiated a pilot test (in March 2004) to gain learner feedback on the redesigned course materials and the logistics of program implementation. The six-month-long pilot test included all phases of managing a distance education program: marketing, matriculation, orientation, course delivery, learner assessment, instructor feedback, and participant evaluations.

To advertise the program, members MUDEP traveled to individual schools in and around the area of Mzuzu University. Prospective participants were given brochures about the program and an application form. The pilot test included evaluations of the application process, a program sensitization seminar, assigning of textbooks and modules, and of course learner assessment and feedback. The program had twenty-eight applicants from fourteen schools. Of the schools, four were Community Day Secondary Schools, six were government schools, and four were private schools. All were within 120 kilometers of Mzuzu's campus. Twenty-five participants were selected for the program. Participants did not pay for any courses during the pilot phase and they were given books for use during the courses. The MUDEP team assured the participants that successful completion of the pilot course would count toward the diploma program itself. Although some of those enrolled wondered about increases in salary given a higher level of training, such decisions are a function of the Ministry of Education, and that issue would have to be settled in later negotiations between higher-level administrators and government officials.

The course delivery phase of the pilot project, rather than being Web-based as initially proposed, was carried out in a manner similar to other correspondence courses. Because it was a pilot test, however, participants were randomly assigned to one of the five modules, thus giving each course instructor approximately five enrollees. The instructors traveled to the participants' work locations at relatively frequent intervals (totaling to about six times during the course) to give and receive instructional feedback. This task was in addition to the MUDEP members' regular duties as lecturers or library staff at the university.

Participants took one of five modules. All reported that they were generally satisfied with the courses and all said they were challenged by the content. Each instructor collected formative evaluation data to be used to refine future iterations of the modules. The following section summarizes the evaluations of two classes based on the pilot test data.

Feedback on Selected Courses. Each course participant enrolled in the courses was a full-time teacher. As such, the factor of having enough time to complete the requirements was a constant challenge. Within the Advanced Educational Psychology course and the Introduction to Educational Research course, two participants dropped out. Their reason given was due primarily to the demands of their job, and not due to the course structure. If they had had more time, then it is possible they could have completed the work. Concerns they expressed about the course content itself ranged from lack of confidence in their ability to write and summarize (particularly if their background was in science or math and not language) and the fact that many text examples made distinctly North American references. Other issues of concern were related to instructor feedback and accessibility of resources for doing a research report. In the first case, it was difficult for the instructors to get to the participants' location with any frequency given the logistical challenges of travel. Access by phone also presented challenges, as in remote parts of Malawi there are few land lines, and cell service is not as good as it is in the urban centers. The need for responsive instructor feedback was particularly felt in project-based courses that emphasize process rather than rote knowledge of facts (an important component in the ITMA program). Those taking the instructional design module were especially impacted by slow feedback, given that forward progress

NEW DIRECTIONS FOR TEACHING AND LEARNING • DOI: 10.1002/tl

could only happen once a given aspect of their design project (e.g., creating learning objectives) met instructor approval. Related to the issue of access to instructors is the issue of obtaining learning materials outside of what is presented in the class text. For a course in educational research, where participants were keen to read other materials, they did not have physical or electronic access to materials that are readily available via the Internet in many other places. All participants were asked about the possibility of doing more than one course in a given semester, and they were unanimous in their opinion that doing so would be impossible given their workload.

Recommendations Based on the Pilot Materials. Participant feedback for all courses showed that supplementary, instructor-created text should be used, in part, to explain textbook-based examples that are exclusive to a U.S. or North American perspective. The question about fees and course-related expenses also touches on textbooks. Grant funding paid for the texts used in the pilot phase. Who would replace these, and at what cost? Some of the texts are very expensive, even by U.S. standards. An additional consideration then becomes whether the MUDEP team would continue to use texts, some of which are now going out of circulation as newer editions become available, or if they will place all course material in instructor-created workbooks. Should instructors have to create their own textbooks (provided they had access to subject matter experts), the development time would undoubtedly delay any courses offered by the program.

Another instructional design issue that is impacted by logistics concerns assessment of participant work. Web-based courses in ITMA program at Virginia Tech rely on participant-created projects for the bulk of assessment. A group of highly educated and trained graduate assistants and faculty use high-speed networks to offer regular feedback on such projects. When the entire system slows down as a result of print-based media and reliance on transportation, the feedback necessary for such projects starts to suffer. For example, participants in courses like the Educational Research module and Principles of Instructional Design module benefited from quick feedback. The inability to support distance students in a way that helps them succeed and learn the materials can be quite frustrating. Therefore, the actual instructional design decisions with regard to assessment need to account for differences in feedback. One possible solution would be to transform the assessment into a less-than-desirable test format; a more expensive option would be to hire tutors.

Factors to Consider in the Redesign Process. The following is not a set of recommendations, as generalizing from such a specific case study is impossible. The project did, however, provide lessons learned, out of which grew the following list of implications. We provide these for designers who might see them as having some bearing on their own efforts to contextualize instruction.

Adaptation requires negotiation. Every level of the redesign project involved negotiation. Negotiating outcomes began at the international level between the funding agencies and educational institutions, and went all the way down to the give and take of those working together to redesign individual courses. The ability to compromise is the key to allowing the adaptation and adoption process to happen naturally.

"Process context" is as important as local context. The goal of the redesign efforts was to use local contextual factors to create courses that could be used in Malawi. However, it is also true that a process context also has a shaping influence in the design of the courses. Factors such as project expectations, perceptions of design or editorial roles, teamwork and communication, as well as time, all make up the process context. These factors influence design just as much as factors in the local context do.

Infrastructure drives instructional design decisions. Well-designed instruction is undoubtedly important. In the redesign of courses, though, it was not instructional design theory or best practices that shaped the adaptation efforts. The focus on infrastructure—what was possible, what was not possible, and what was unknown—shaped design decisions almost exclusively.

Good message design in one format is not the best for another. One area of design that did not receive a lot of attention during the project was related to layout of the materials. This is an important element of instructional design. The technologies that would have brought about a more print-friendly format went unused. Just as Web-based courses should be designed to be more than a simple replication of text-based materials, the same should be true in reverse.

Instructional designers need to talk about theoretical issues. It cannot be assumed that designers will focus on the ramifications of theory on their work or in their work. Shambaugh and Magliaro (1997) write, "Learning beliefs are frequently embedded in the complex contexts of real settings where the values and beliefs of schools, businesses, and communities must be considered" (p. 4). They go on to assert that making one's beliefs known and comparing them to design components allows a designer to "remain vigilant that [his or her] beliefs are addressed appropriately for the nature of the content, the needs of the learners, and the realities of the instructional setting" (p. 4). In this project, designers tended to focus on practical issues related to logistics. Their redesign efforts tended to focus on generally surface-level features. This does not mean that their work had no theoretical relevance. Opportunities for a discussion about designers' personal theoretical orientations, as well as a discussion on the assumptions inherent in courses selected for redesign, should be sought.

Challenges and Considerations

As noted earlier, the course materials were not the only piece adapted for local needs. In fact, it could be argued that the material itself went relatively unchanged compared to the much larger programmatic and logistical considerations. For example, one could argue that even expertly designed content that cannot be delivered due to lack of infrastructure does less good than North American- or U.K.-centric materials that are made available to participants in a convenient manner. The main challenges did not lie in re-examining the course content per se, but in trying to determine the ways by which the broader project goals might be accomplished. When one takes away a potentially scalable solution such as network storage and delivery of materials, and a mode of immediate (or close to immediate) feedback via electronic communications, then there emerges a cascading set of factors that automatically impact design decisions. Attempts to internationalize meet logistical requirements head on. A common assumption in the field of instructional design is that one cannot let the technology tools drive the curriculum—that the design and content must come first. This is a wise approach for the novice, but the expert designer must closely account for how a grand design will ultimately be delivered.

The impact on pedagogy is no less. Take, for instance, the notion of creating a project-based course versus one where students read material from a chapter and then are tested on it. In a context where immediate feedback is possible, doing project-based classes makes sense as students can engage in problems and get input from peers and facilitators on a consistent basis. However, if the context is such that this is not possible, a class based on multiple-choice tests, where knowledge is never transferred into something tangible, although not the preferred mode, may well be the only mode feasible. The program may have lofty goals of promoting student-centered, social constructivist environments, but are those achievable? The answer is "it depends," the mantra of instructional technologists the world over.

Internationalization by Systematic Design

One could characterize the internationalized facets of the program as being emic, or "from within," rather than being a program mandate that guided how revisions should proceed. Because each design team had a Malawian colleague as a member, they were looked upon as the ultimate judges of whether or not the materials fit the context in which they would be used. Every step of the process, starting with a needs assessment, all the way to the pilot testing of materials and the roll-out of the postgraduate diploma program, involved input from and collaboration with the students from Malawi. Being able to understand first-hand knowledge of local needs was a critical factor throughout the project.

Although the term "internationalization" was not a formal part of the revision and transitioning process, objectives typically identified with it were always an inherent part of the conversations guiding the systematic process of design. As Schoorman (2000) writes, "as an ongoing process, internationalization entails the constant monitoring of and adaptation to the changing needs and demands of the global and local context" (p. 26). Instructional design, which is by nature systematic and reiterative, provides a framework to carry out the steps further identified by Schoorman: planning, identification of global and local changes, creation of long-range and short-term goals, and the evaluation of those goals (p. 26). It might be said then, that facets of internationalization can take place without a top-down, or even explicit mandate for it. Engaging people in the process of design, where the goals of contextualization are present in the problem-solving environment, can bring out perspectives and concerns related to internationalization in a manner that is natural, collegial, and responsive.

References

Dean, G. *Designing Instruction for Adult Learners.* Malabar, FL: Krieger, 1990.

Schoorman, D. *Internationalization: The Challenge of Implementing Organizational Rhetoric* (ED 444 427). Boca Raton: Florida Atlantic University, 2000.

Shambaugh, R. N., and Magliaro, S. G. *Mastering the Possibilities: A Process Approach to Instructional Design.* Boston: Allyn and Bacon, 1997.

Tessmer, M. "Environment Analysis: A Neglected State of Instructional Design." *Educational Technology, Research and Development,* 1990, *38*(1), 55–64.

Tessmer, M., and Harris, D. *Analysing the Instructional Setting.* London: Kogan Page Ltd., 1992.

Tessmer, M., and Richey, R. "The Role of Context in Learning and Instructional Design." *Educational Technology, Research and Development,* 1997, *45*(2), 85–115.

Tiene, D., and Futagami, S. "Designing Effective Educational Multimedia Projects: General Guidelines for Developing Countries." *International Journal of Instructional Media,* 1987, *14*(4), 282–292.

ROSS A. PERKINS *is a senior project associate in the Office of Educational Research and Outreach in the School of Education at Virginia Tech.*

9

Internationalization of the curriculum needs to be connected to a pedagogical discussion to be transformative.

Internationalizing Curriculum: A New Kind of Education?

Arja Vainio-Mattila

In this chapter, I will examine some of the shifts that are informing our understanding of what "internationalizing curriculum" might mean for the small undergraduate liberal arts college at which I teach in London, Ontario. I will start by describing an initiative that was developed to allow students studying a profoundly "international" curriculum to learn outside the classroom, locally. I will then attempt to explain how internationalizing the curriculum is viewed generally in higher education in Canada today. Finally, I will attempt to demonstrate how important it is for the discussion on internationalizing curriculum to become more connected to pedagogical debates.

In 2000, Huron University College had a relatively new, but rapidly growing program that was housed in a department called the Centre for International Studies. The Centre offered a number of academic modules, most of which were identified by "international," as in International Development Studies, International and Comparative Studies, and International Culture Studies. The courses largely used material that was recognizably international, that is to say, case studies from outside Canada, authors from the regions being studied, and discourse analysis of how the world is viewed, or the international constructed. Among this material was also a whole body of knowledge on the First Nations of Canada. Realization that international existed within Canada was one impetus to begin questioning that concept. The courses at the Centre also engaged intensively with issues

NEW DIRECTIONS FOR TEACHING AND LEARNING, no. 118, Summer 2009 © Wiley Periodicals, Inc.
Published online in Wiley InterScience (www.interscience.wiley.com) • DOI: 10.1002/tl.356

such as poverty, globalization, migration, and international development, which further led to the questions, "Do we study these only as they pertain to the 'international'?" "In fact, to what extent does Canada itself represent the 'international'?"

The "Think Global, Act Local" (TGAL) initiative was launched in 2001 to create an opportunity, integrated in the academic curriculum, for students to engage locally in the global issues they studied. TGAL was offered as a course for which the student participants received academic credit and which contributed to several degree options at the Centre. TGAL was based on strong partnerships with civil society organizations working on global issues in the London (Ontario) area. Over a five-year period students worked on immigration and refugee, environmental, poverty, First Nations, HIV/AIDS, and violence against women issues, and they worked on international development. The challenge was to develop a program which would create a realistic partnership between our undergraduate students and civil society organizations with often limited resources to address significant issues. The task was to identify activities appropriate for undergraduate students to engage in, while ensuring that the supervisory expectations we had of the community partners did not imperil their main activities.

Description of the Initiative

The "Think Global, Act Local" initiative began in the academic year of 2001–2002 as a pilot program for third-year students at the Centre for International Studies. The participants in the course were chosen on the basis of an application in which the applicants were invited to discuss their areas of interest, contributions, and possible matches with local non-governmental organizations (NGOs). In taking this one-term course, students made a commitment to volunteer at least three hours a week during the academic term of their time with a London-based NGO addressing a local manifestation of a global issue. The students were expected to use their skills in information identification and organization to produce an output that was useful to the partner organization (see Table 9.1). It is important to know that the students were not expected to work as frontline workers for the partner organizations, but rather to provide services based on skills in which undergraduate students are well versed. In addition, the students were expected to produce an academic paper on the particular initiatives their placement organization engaged in. This paper provided the basis for the course grade.

There were three partners in this venture at Huron: the students, the non-governmental organization, and the instructor. The instructor was a professor at the Centre who taught this course as a half course out of an expected three full-course normal teaching load in each term. Each partner had a specific role in the collaboration.

NEW DIRECTIONS FOR TEACHING AND LEARNING • DOI: 10.1002/tl

Table 9.1. Examples of Student Engagements 2001–2005

Type of organization	Examples of student products for the non-governmental organizations
Cultural organizations	Production of teachers' materials on refugees in Canada Production of teachers' materials on fair trade Information searches on indigenous peoples' health issues Locating funding sources
Health organizations	Cataloguing HIV/AIDS materials Mapping resources for women re-establishing independent lives for themselves and their children in London Research on impact of violence on children in Rwanda
Poverty organizations	Food security programs Public education Developing website
Environmental organizations	Research on resources related to homelessness Conducting research for the facilitation of clean air campaign Research for water/sovereignty campaign
Human rights organizations	Developing database on activities of the organization in El Salvador Developing educational module on International Humanitarian Law Anti-racism campaign Research on resistance struggles of indigenous people in Columbia Development of educational media for public presentations Development of online mentorship

We asked the student to:

- Make a commitment of at least three hours a week to the NGO in question.
- Produce a written piece of work that would meet an identified information need of the NGO. This could be, for example, a fact sheet, a brochure, or text for Web pages.
- Produce a research essay (5000 words) and an annotated bibliography on a topic related to the focus of the NGO activities.

We asked the NGO to:

- Provide opportunity for a student to learn about the operation of their organization.
- Work in partnership with the student on a project that serves the NGO's information need.
- Evaluate the student and success of partnership upon completion of the course.

And the instructor was responsible for:

- Overseeing the joint venture between the student and the NGO from its inception to its completion.
- Supervising and grading of the work required for completion of the course and work completed for the NGO.

The "Think Global, Act Local" initiative was unique in our institution because of the way it was integrated into the academic curriculum. There are many examples in Canadian universities of internship programs whose goals relate to development of specific skills, and volunteer programs that are outside the curriculum. "Think Global, Act Local" was a course that explored how global issues are played out within a Canadian context. As such, it both addressed a key concern of the Centre that students have the opportunity to realize that the international characteristic of human life is not only a product of international relationships, but a profound underlying current of their everyday lives in Canada, and engaged with the Huron ethos of promoting internationalization and service.

The "Think Global, Act Local" was a very popular course if measured by student interest. Yet, for the last two years the course has not been offered even though it still remains on the books and Huron has expressed a strong interest in offering it in the future. After the initial pilot of two years, the course grew to accommodate student interest and evolved into an academically more demanding one with required reading and seminars in addition to the written work. The challenges faced in continually offering such a course are partly, or even mostly, resource based. To identify and maintain ongoing community partnerships, when done well, is an extremely time-consuming affair, and beyond the scope of most instructors working within a normal teaching and research load. More interesting, and challenging to resolve, are the fundamental questions the course raised about the relationship of Huron University College with the community it inhabits; the relationships between international, local, and global, as well as the pedagogical issues of experiential learning, community-based learning, and service learning; and finally the apparent disconnect between these pedagogical debates and the strategies of internationalization. These questions invite me as an educator to step back from the success and failure stories of specific initiatives to re-examine what exactly is the nature of pedagogical engagement in internationalization.

Context for Internationalization Initiatives

The TGAL initiative at Huron contributed to a new communal understanding that the "international" is highly problematic because of the difficulty of locating the many, and multidimensional, connections between international places and London (Ontario) with regard to the issues faculty and students at the Centre were studying. Partially as a result of this contribution, the Centre was renamed the Centre for Global Studies, framing the discourse in terms of scale (local to global) rather than place ("here," "there"). Having participated in the discussions that precipitated the shift, I was left wondering what contribution could this shift make to the more general discussion on internationalization in higher education.

But I am getting ahead of myself, for there is a more mainstream understanding of internationalization in which little shift has taken place. Internationalization of higher education is often viewed in terms of a process aimed at reaching a state of internationalization. This is depicted by goals measuring international student and faculty mobility, international research contacts, and provision of campus-based services for the "international," i.e., pre-departure briefings for students, English as second language training, workshops for international faculty, and so on. Strategic plans make reference to qualitative goals of international experience sought by students and to global commitment (University of Western Ontario, 2006), but the concrete strategic commitments are articulated in terms of quantifiable programs. Jane Knight's 2000 *AUCC Report on Internationalization at Canadian Universities* attempts to stretch this understanding by suggesting that internationalization should be viewed as the continuing process of integrating an international and intercultural perspective into the teaching, learning, research, and service functions of higher education. This definition reflects the practice that often exists at the intersection of the international and intercultural. She originally coined this definition in 1995 (Knight, 1995), and it is reconfirmed in the most recent report on internationalization in Canada (Association of Universities and Colleges of Canada [AUCC], 2007) which states, "In the higher education context, internationalization is understood as the process of integrating an international and intercultural dimension to teaching/learning, research and service functions of a university" (p. 1).

The 2007 AUCC survey on internationalization in Canada collated the results into the five categories of international student mobility, internationalization of curriculum, knowledge exports, Canadian university engagement in development cooperation, and international research. These represent the quantifiable areas of engagement with internationalization. The report is extensive and useful in identifying trends in the field of internationalization, but raises few questions about the underlying pedagogical assumptions regarding the motivation of this engagement. In general terms, it is interesting to note that there has been significant growth in organizational resources directed towards internationalization, some growth in offering programs that identify an international focus, modest growth in Canadian students going abroad to study (some campuses now reach over 10% internationalization of their student body, while nationally the proportion of Canadian students going abroad is closer to 2%), and an actual downturn in numbers of universities requiring students to study a second language (AUCC, 2007). (This latter trend directly contradicts a rhetorical commitment to integrate international and intercultural dimensions into curricula.) It is very difficult to get a similar quantitative picture of whether students as a result of internationalization now increasingly contextualize whatever they are studying in an interconnected, global world.

It is also impossible to discuss internationalization of higher education without reference to the parallel discourse on experiential learning, or service learning, or community-based learning as it is alternatively called. Both the discourses on internationalization and on experiential learning emerge from pressures, both internal and external, that universities face today to connect the experience of learning in a university with the world outside the ivory tower. There is a general expectation that universities should better prepare students for the "real world" through development of both mind sets and skills sets that will serve them post-graduation.

However, whereas the push to internationalize is relatively recent as a widespread phenomenon in universities, experiential learning has a longer history in the form of internships, practicum training, volunteerism, cooperative placement, and so on. It is also informed by a fuller discourse about fundamentals such as how diversification of the student body, or learning through partnerships, or understanding connections between theory and praxis impacts academic pursuits (Galura and others, 2004). On internationalization there is still a gap in such literature, although work evaluating specific programs (e.g., Odgers and Giroux, 2006) or aspects of programs such as the nature of international volunteerism (Tiessen and Heron, 2007) has started to emerge. In fact, as the universities have begun to push for increasing linkages with partners in other countries, those voices critical of imbalances inherent especially in partnerships that inhabit the North–South axis have found little space to express these concerns in the context of internationalization.

International Is Both Global and Local

More important than the mechanics of how internationalization is delivered, however, is a discussion about the possibility of embedding it in a critical pedagogy that seeks to guide the student to understand herself or himself as an active agent in society as well as to identify and create conditions for a more just society—in other words, anchoring the process of internationalization in the core educational mission of higher education rather than presenting it as a delivery mechanism. bell hooks (2003) writes about a "pedagogical revolution" that challenges the institutionalized systems of domination. This concept is relevant if internationalization is to be understood as a forum of such change. Curriculum development in general, and internationalization of curriculum in particular, present us with critical opportunities to create the "new kind of education" described by hooks (2003).

In considering what could be the pedagogical imperatives of this "new kind of education," I am drawn further to the points made by hooks about what we could learn from previous iterations of such fundamental pedagogical shifts. She writes, "The feminist challenge to patriarchal curriculum and patriarchal teaching practices completely altered the classroom. . . . Students often flocked in droves to feminist classrooms because schooling there was simply more academically compelling" (hooks, 2003, pp. 4–5).

This insight on the transformative power of feminist pedagogy is an invitation to learn about how higher education curriculum has been changed in recent history. Can internationalization of the curriculum challenge the status quo of global relationships in such a way as to alter the experience of learning? What will be so compelling about the "internationalized" that students will flock in droves to engage with this experience? hooks further challenges the idea that going away will in itself somehow better prepare students for life after university. She writes:

> Teachers who have a vision of democratic education assume that learning is never confined solely to an institutionalized classroom. Rather than embodying the conventional false assumption that the university setting is not the 'real world' and teaching accordingly, the democratic educator breaks through the false construction of the corporate university as set apart of our real world experience, and our real life. Embracing the concept of a democratic education we see teaching and learning as taking place constantly. We share the knowledge gleaned in classrooms beyond those settings thereby working to challenge the construction of certain forms of knowledge as always and only available to the elite (hooks, 2003, p. 41).

Although hooks is not writing specifically in reference to internationalization, her writing presents an astute critique of the institutionalized processes of internationalization: student mobility may move students to a different setting, but does it impact how they learn? There may be more opportunities for international engagement, but they are primarily accessed by a very small (elite) group of students. How can we explore the potential for using the opportunities implied by the opening up of higher education institutions through internationalization not just to change the place of education, but to help understand the connections between the locale we inhabit, and the other localities, as contributors to a global truly radicalizing the teaching/learning relationship?

To increase the impact of internationalization of the curriculum on the educational experience, we need to focus perhaps less on quantitative indicators of student mobility and more on creation of communities of learning that involve diverse inhabitants of various localities and multiple scales of globality. And we may want to draw on ideas of democratic education or Freirean pedagogy (Freire, 1971) to frame learning in such a way that our students have a chance of not only becoming good (read *compliant*) global citizens, but agents of change actively pursuing more equal and just relationships that may or may not be international but are always global.

This chapter arises largely from fear that internationalization as it is now commonly constructed is an opportunity wasted. It is possible that all kinds of benefits accrue to the institutions involved from such an exercise, and that individual students may indeed benefit, but as an educational experience, it seems to me that it is narrowly defined and consequently limited in its appeal. In fact, I am struck by the relevance of an anecdote told by Beckham (2004) in his discussion on diversity as an educational imperative. He recalls an address by the Dean of Admissions at Wesleyan in which he said, "Wesleyan needs black students in order to educate white students." Internationalization in higher education is in grave danger of becoming another avenue by which an elite group of students accesses the world for their benefit. Instead, internationalizing curriculum should be grounded in the educational mission of the institutions.

For example, like most higher education institutions, Huron University College (HUC) identifies as its principal academic objectives:

> . . . to promote educational excellence, to encourage scholarly achievement, to foster international understanding and co-operation, and to provide its students with a broad and useful education that will develop their intellectual skills, enhance their desire for knowledge, and prepare them for positions of leadership and responsibility (HUC, 2007).

Accordingly, we see our students not only leaving the college and doing their part in the world outside the academic setting, we see them as taking on positions of leadership. We see them as challenging that world from whatever place they inhabit because of their critical engagement with the global while at the college. Programs such as the "Think Global, Act Local," offered locally or internationally, can be key tools in this process. Through them, students are involved in a community of learning that embraces both the university and outside, and through their engagement with the global in the local context, they can in fact have a truly "international" learning experience.

It may be overstretching it to suggest that programs such as TGAL at Huron offer every bit an authentic way of learning about the international as any study abroad experience, but I would suggest, in conclusion, that it is crucial to apply the lessons learned in such programs to rethinking how we approach the internationalized components of curricula. There should be space for program innovation offered by universities to be informed by theoretical innovation in pedagogy.

References

Association of Universities and Colleges of Canada (AUCC). *Internationalizing Canadian Campuses: Main Themes Emerging from the 2007 Scotiabank-AUCC Workshop on Excellence in Internationalization at Canadian Universities.* Ottawa: AUCC, Scotiabank, 2007.
Beckham, E. "Diversity: An Educational Imperative." In J. A. Galura, P. A. Pasque, D. Schoem, and J. Howard (eds.), *Engaging the Whole of Service Learning, Diversity and Learning Communities.* Ann Arbor: OCSL Press, 2004.

Freire, P. *Pedagogy of the Oppressed.* New York: Continuum, 1971.

Galura, J. A., Pasque, P. A., Schoen, D., and Howard, J. (Eds.) *Engaging the Whole of Service-Learning, Diversity, and Learning Communities.* Ann Arbor, MI: The OCSL Press at the University of Michigan, 2004.

hooks, b. *Teaching Community: A Pedagogy of Hope.* London/New York: Routledge, 2003.

Huron University College (HUC). Mission statement. http://www.huronuc.ca/about_huron/more_about_huron/mission_statement/. Accessed January 20, 2008.

Knight, J. *Internationalization of Canadian Universities: The Changing Landscape.* Ottawa: Association of Universities and Colleges of Canada, 1995.

Knight, J. *Progress and Promise: The 2000 AUCC Report on Internationalization at Canadian Universities.* Ottawa: Association of Universities and Colleges of Canada, 2000.

Odgers, T., and Giroux, I. "Internationalizing Faculty: A Phased Approach to Transforming Curriculum Design and Instruction." Presented at the York University Annual International Conference on Internationalizing Canada's Universities, March 2–3, 2006.

Tiessen, R., and Heron, B. Creating Global Citizens: Impact of Volunteer and Work Abroad Programs. Ottawa, Ontario: International Development Research Centre, Canada, 2007.

University of Western Ontario (UWO). "Engaging the Future: 5. Internationalization." Final Report of the Task Force on Strategic Planning. http://www.uwo.ca/pvp/strategic_pla/report/05.htm. Accessed January 2008.

ARJA VAINIO-MATTILA is the associate dean of Huron University College where she is also an associate professor of Global Development Studies at the Centre for Global Studies.

NEW DIRECTIONS FOR TEACHING AND LEARNING • DOI: 10.1002/tl

Universities can contribute to a vision of global sustainability through research, teaching, and acting as models in their own physical operations. This chapter examines the role universities can and must play in achieving global sustainability and how this relates to the internationalization of the institution.

Sustainability, Internationalization, and Higher Education

Tarah S. A. Wright

In the late twentieth and early twenty-first century, humanity has become more aware of a multitude of global environmental problems that threaten human and ecosystem health. The perceived ramifications of environmental degradation has led many governments and international agencies to highlight the necessity for society to adopt the principles of sustainable development and the need for individuals to be educated in a way that leads to a sustainable future. The concept of education for sustainable development (ESD) has become so important that the United Nations declared 2005–2014 the United Nations Decade of Education for Sustainable Development. Universities are recognized as key institutions that contribute to the vision of a global sustainable future through research, teaching, and acting as models of sustainability in their own physical operations. In this chapter, I will discuss the role universities can and must play in achieving global sustainability and how this relates to the internationalization of the institution.

Conceptualizing Sustainable Development

The term *sustainable development* became known among the international environmental community in 1972 at the United Nations Conference on the Human Environment. The occasion that arguably brought the term into common use worldwide was the World Commission on Environment and

NEW DIRECTIONS FOR TEACHING AND LEARNING, no. 118, Summer 2009 © Wiley Periodicals, Inc.
Published online in Wiley InterScience (www.interscience.wiley.com) • DOI: 10.1002/tl.357

Development (WCED), which defined sustainable development as "meeting the needs of the present without compromising the ability of future generations to meet their own needs" (WCED, 1987, p. 43). Similar sentiments were echoed at the United Nations Conference on Environment and Development (1992), and the World Summit on Sustainable Development in Johannesburg (2002). The main tenets of sustainable development are a focus on integrating ecological, economic, and social considerations into decision making; intergenerational equity; increasing equity within nations and among developed and developing countries (intragenerational equity); reducing population growth; and conserving and enhancing the resource base.

It is important to note that sustainable development does not focus solely on the natural environment (although it is commonly seen as such, and is often portrayed as being about the natural environment in political rhetoric). Many of you may be familiar with the more popular conceptualization of sustainable development (see Figure 10.1) in which the "triple bottom line," or "three interdependent and mutually reinforcing pillars" of sustainability, have been satisfied. According to this view of sustainable development, the three circles of economic development, social development, and environmental protection come together. The intersection of these is where sustainable development occurs.

According to this understanding of sustainable development, decision makers seek strategies to optimize social, economic, and environmental conditions simultaneously.

Critics of this conceptualization feel that it is based on highly dubious assumptions. For example, the text accompanying this model states that an integral aspect of sustainable development is the development of poorer, less developed countries to the standards of "developed" (I often think of them as overdeveloped) nations. On the surface, this can be viewed as an admirable task; however, it totally disregards the carrying capacity of the earth and the earth's ability to produce even the basic needs of the current global human population. Ecological footprint models (see works by Wackenagel and Reese for more information) demonstrate that it is physically impossible for the earth to produce all of the goods North Americans consume for every person on the earth. According to footprint calculations, humanity would need at least three planets the size of our earth for all of humanity to attain the lifestyle of North Americans and live in a way that does not compromise the earth's ecosystems. A great misconception perpetuated by this model is that we can alleviate world poverty and solve social problems through the expansion of the use of world resources rather than a more equitable distribution of current resources. This would cause those living in developed nations to change the way they live fundamentally and to reassess the basic tenets of their current economic model.

To address these criticisms, new models of sustainability have been developed that give a better conceptualization of our ecological reality. For example, Prescott-Allen (2001) demonstrates a hierarchically organized "egg

Figure 10.1. Common Conceptualization of Sustainable Development

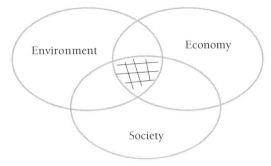

Source: Adapted from World Commission on Environment and Development (WCED), 1987.

of sustainability" (see Figure 10.2). This model illustrates the relationship between humans and the ecosystem as one circle inside another. This model demonstrates that humans reside within the global ecosystem, and emphasizes that we are entirely dependent upon the ecosystem for our well-being. Although this is a well-known scientific fact, it radically deviates from many perceptions of humanity as being somehow separate from nature. In the egg of sustainability, the economy is considered only one subsystem of the human system (others include health and well-being, governance, knowledge, community) and is thus not given equal weighting as is the impression given in the traditional model (Figure 10.1). Society is only sustainable

Figure 10.2. The Egg of Sustainability

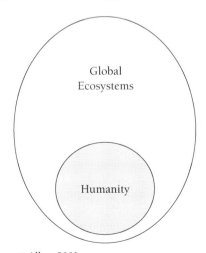

Source: Adapted from Prescott-Allen, 2001.

if both the human system and ecosystem are healthy (i.e., the white and yolk of the egg must both be healthy for the whole system to be robust). This schematic places social and economic development as subordinate to the global ecosystem.

Such conceptualizations of sustainable development are naturally international in scope. For example, one cannot talk about the influence of air pollution on human health and reproduction from a country standpoint. Air pollution does not respect geo-political borders, but is rather indiscriminate in who it affects. Nor can one discuss current social conflicts and war without addressing the influences of global inequities in creating such hostilities. In reality, society and the environment must be healthy globally for humanity to claim that we are living sustainably.

The Role of the University in Creating a Global Sustainable Future

Although a global sustainable future cannot be achieved through changes in one sector alone, higher education in particular is seen as a vehicle to work towards this goal. Higher education is recognized as having a moral responsibility to become physical models of sustainability and centers of sustainability research and teaching expertise. As Clugston (1999) explains, universities are vested by society with the task of discerning truth, imparting values, and socializing students to contribute to social progress and the advancement of knowledge. Higher education has a major responsibility to impart the moral vision and technical knowledge needed to ensure a high quality of life for future generations. According to the United Nations Educational, Scientific and Cultural Organization (UNESCO), "the goal of (higher) education is to make people wiser, more knowledgeable, better informed, ethical, responsible, critical and capable of continuing to learn. . . . Education, in short, is humanity's best hope and most effective means in the quest to achieve sustainable development" (UNESCO, 1997).

However, universities in industrialized nations in particular have been criticized for their unsustainable behavior. Perhaps the best known critic is David Orr who argues that sustainability problems are not the work of ignorant people, but "largely the result of work by people with BA's, B.Sc.'s, LLB's, MBA's and PhD's" (Orr, 1995, p. 7). Ecological footprint models show us that the well-educated people of the industrialized countries of the world use the majority of the earth's natural resources and contribute the most to the world's sustainability problems. In fact, many scholars criticize higher education for producing disciplinary leaders incapable of addressing critical sustainability problems because they are blindly contributing to them.

Unfortunately, I have made similar observations in my own life. One of my favorite examples is from a trip I took to Toronto a number of years back. I was in the downtown business center taking an elevator up to see some old school friends who were working at a high-powered law firm. In the elevator, I overheard three lawyers talking about a government proposal to sell water from Lake Ontario to the United States. One of the lawyers said "let them take it – who would want to drink water from Lake Ontario anyhow?" The reaction from the other two lawyers was laughter and agreement. It was very difficult for me to not turn to them and ask them where they thought the water in their taps came from. None was aware that City of Toronto tap water, which services over 3 million people a day, comes from Lake Ontario. It was staggering to know that these highly educated individuals with at least two degrees each had such limited understanding of the world around them.

I have also made these observations within my university. It seems that the academy is very good at fragmenting and sectoralizing information so that one discipline has no understanding of its impact on the other. For example, I teach a mandatory first year environmental science class to students enrolled in the Bachelor of Management program. The students in this program regularly come to the first day of class without any enthusiasm or interest in the subject matter. Many of these students have said to me that they do not see how an environmental science class can help them in the business world. If these students did not take my class, they would graduate from the university understanding only the economic implications of their activities. For example, students would understand the financial benefits of extracting oil from the ground, but not the full environmental and social ramifications and costs. Though I do my best to teach these students that business ventures usually have social, environmental, and economic impacts, it is disappointing that most students simply do not care. To many of them, economics represents the bottom line. This is perpetuated by the rhetoric heard in developed countries and seems to have become a societal norm. In the end, most people believe that environmental and social problems are for someone else to deal with. If environmental degradation were to occur on a global level (there is evidence to support that this is currently happening), most of the students in the Bachelor of Management program would state that they will be able to continue to live their privileged lives and that it will be the poor in non-industrialized nations who will be affected.

These examples are only two of many that give a clear indication that our universities are graduating ecologically illiterate students who are not prepared to help pave the way to a sustainable future. This is a true failure of our entire education system on many levels. First, it is a failure to teach holistic and realistic curriculum that conforms to the laws of nature and the tenets of sustainable development. Business students are taught that linear growth is essential to economic prosperity. They are not taught that it is the earth's biological infrastructure that makes possible our human infrastructure. They are not taught the finite limits of both non-renewable resources such as oil, and renewable resources such as forests (if production exceeds biological and physical abilities to regenerate). They are not taught about the well-known scientifically valid ecological footprint model that shows that the earth's biological capacity (the total biological production capacity per year of a biologically productive space) cannot support humanity's current consumption and waste production. They are not taught that we are liquidating natural capital to support current resource use, reducing the Earth's ability to support future life (thus negating the key sustainable development concept of inter-generational equity). Although the curriculum should teach that growing human consumption demands can no longer be met by tapping unexploited resources, these scientific findings are often ignored.

Second, it is my belief that by teaching in a fragmented and sectoralized way, universities are failing to develop moral human beings. For students to engage in such individualistic thinking so as to not care how their actions may negatively impact people in less-developed countries is contrary to one of the original purposes of the university: to develop socially responsible citizens. For higher education to truly address sustainability problems and educate the citizenry to move toward sustainability, a fundamental re-thinking of the purpose of the university and how we teach is needed.

A New University Mission: Global Sustainability

What is the raison d'etre of the university? Although there are some variations in interpretation, Brubacher (1982) suggests two philosophies underlying the functions of the modern university. The first is epistemological in nature; it states that the university's purpose is to answer the great questions of human existence. According to this philosophy, universities seek knowledge and truth. Alternatively, the political philosophy of education states that universities not only seek knowledge, but also apply the knowledge to solve the complex problems of society. The university educates the citizenry, and prepares students for an active life and social responsibility in the world. Scott (2006) further suggests that universities are rapidly heading toward a new paradigm of purpose. He claims that as nation-states become increasingly interdependent, a new university mission is arising: internationalization. According to Scott, the internationalization of the university mission does not mean doing away with the existing missions of the university, but changing the focus to the international stage.

Combining the existing university mission of solving complex societal problems with this new paradigm of internationalization naturally leads to a focus on global sustainability, as there is no social problem greater than that of ensuring human survival on the planet. I am not alone in this assertion. Scholars from around the world (including 108 Nobel Laureates) feel that humanity's future is bleak at best, and that all other human issues become moot if sustainability is not addressed immediately.

Moving the Agenda Forward

Given this proposed new paradigm for the university, how can we in higher education work towards creating a global sustainable future? One suggestion is to make a class on sustainable development mandatory for all students who graduate from a university. Some institutions, like Florida Gulf Coast University and Evergreen State College in the United States have embraced this concept. Although I understand the reasoning behind the suggestion, I am not a proponent of such initiatives. There may be some positive aspects to having all students take a course to learn about their surrounding environment and its influences on humanity; however, by making a course mandatory, there are two possible negative outcomes.

First, such a class may create resentment among the student population. As was the case with my Bachelor of Management students, students in disciplines that traditionally have not focused on sustainability issues will likely say, "I don't understand why we have to take this course—it has nothing to do with our degree." Second, a mandatory class serves to isolate issues of sustainability. A single class reinforces the notion that environment and sustainability are special interests rather than something to be considered across the disciplines. Such a course might teach students about the environment and society, but does not contextualize it within their chosen discipline (i.e., what does the environment and sustainability have to do with business, education, or engineering?).

Further, sustainability may not constitute a subject in itself. Rather, ESD provides students with a whole set of knowledge and skills that will lead to a more harmonious relationship among humanity and between humanity and the global ecosystem. Therefore, sustainability cannot be the domain of any one discipline or course. A preliminary move forward would be to infuse sustainability concepts and critical thinking skills into each of the disciplines. This is already being done in cases across the world. *Teaching Sustainability in Universities* (edited by Walter Leal Filho, 2002) is one of many books that offer case studies of how individual professors have incorporated ESD into their classrooms. Examples range from weaving sustainability concepts and skills into a teacher education class, to incorporating sustainability issues into a food science curriculum.

The ultimate goal in ESD, however, is to approach curriculum and program development in a holistic and interdisciplinary way. This is not to say that disciplines should be abolished. Rather, disciplines and university programs should be re-oriented toward creating sustainable solutions for the future with the recognition that sustainability problems cannot be solved by one sector alone.

ESD not only means changing some of the content that we teach, but challenging traditional notions of how to teach. Team teaching is likely essential in achieving effective curriculum for sustainable development. Further, while traditional delivery methods (lecture, lab, and tutorial) serve to inform students, they can been criticized for failing to promote a full understanding or appreciation of sustainability issues as a whole. In the case of my Bachelor of Management students, individuals were able to understand the global environmental and social ramifications of various business ventures by the end of the semester, but still did not seem to care. Educating for sustainable development requires a different approach to teaching so that students translate knowledge into positive action for a global sustainable future.

> No amount of preaching to the citizenry about the perils of a polluted environment, the dangers of irresponsible disposal of wastes or deforestation and the benefit to mankind [sic] of greening the environment will make people act to seek to forestall environmental degradation unless they are imbued with a deep concern for the common good, a sense of responsibility for maintaining a balanced and healthy ecosystem and a strong drive to achieve harmony with nature (UNESCO, 1990, as cited in Clover, Follen, and Hall, 1998).

As mentioned earlier, many scholars believe that our institutions of higher education are failing in that they teach skills and knowledge, yet do not provide a situation where students can adopt positive attitudes towards the environment and society, and therefore graduate ill equipped to deal with sustainability problems. Combining experiential learning and ESD may reverse this trend by helping to develop in students a sense of empathy for society, the natural environment, and an understanding of how to solve sustainability problems through hands-on learning (see Wright, 2006, for more information).

Experiential education is a process for learning through action in which students are engaged in experiences that focus on reflection to increase knowledge, develop skills, and clarify values. Dewey (1960) stressed that students should have the ability to investigate issues within their surroundings and be able to make decisions regarding solutions. Not only did he view education as a basis for societal change, he also felt that experiential activities within an educational setting would lead to behavioral change among students. In essence, he believed that if experience could be made conscious, it could have the ability to be transformative.

Transformative learning theory should also be contemplated as we work toward a global sustainable future. According to Mezirow (1997), transformative learning is the process of effecting change in a frame of reference—that is to say, a change in one's understanding of the world or one's perceptual filters. The educational reformer Freire transcended the idea of transformation from the individual to the social sphere. He criticized the traditional education system for didactically relaying information to students without promoting critical reflection: "Instead of communicating, the teacher issues communiques and makes deposits which the students patiently receive, memorize and repeat" (Freire, 1970, p. 58).

The ideal education system for Freire would see students as co-learners in the process of education and encouraged to engage continuously in praxis (a constant flux between critical reflection and action). This type of education involves conscientization: "a process of developing consciousness, but consciousness that is understood to have the power to transform reality" (Freire, 1970, p. 52). Through conscientization, students are able to recognize the political, social, and economic contradictions in their world and take action to change. It is apparent that the goals of experiential education, transformative learning, and ESD are similar: teaching to change the world and students' perceptions of the world.

A final pedagogical tool that we should not discount in moving towards global sustainability is embedded in how we run our institutions of higher education. Many universities are guilty of unsustainable practices in their physical operations and have thus lost an important educational opportunity to model sustainable behavior. Imagine the pedagogical benefits of erecting self-sufficient buildings on campus that demonstrate "green" technologies, creating close-looped waste management systems, showcasing sustainable transportation on-campus, and providing opportunities for intra-generational equity on campus. Of all the changes that could be made within higher education to reorient it towards ESD, this is arguably the easiest, as making changes in the way a university is run physically is much less contentious than creating changes to how a university is organized academically.

Challenges to Change

Creating these suggested fundamental changes to reorient universities to work towards global sustainability is not an easy road to travel. Many barriers stand in the way. To begin with, issues related to university governance present challenges along the path of sustainability. From a Canadian perspective, external forces influence universities. All Canadian universities derive their powers from provincial legislation and are considered to be legal corporations. Though Canadian universities are considered autonomous institutions, many critics question this notion. In Canada, universities rely on operating grants from their provincial or territorial government to finance the activities of the institution. Such external influences can have a profound effect on the way an institution approaches sustainability issues. Thus, if the political will is not there, the university's hands could be tied. Further, almost all Canadian universities have developed a bicameral governance structure. A Board of Governors represents government and other interests (commonly alumni and students) and is charged with the operation of the university including administrative and financial matters. A senior academic decision-making body (often called the Senate or the General Faculties Council) is responsible for all academic matters including student discipline academic appeals, and approving faculty, tenure, and promotion appointments and programs of study presented by faculties. The President of the University is considered the Chief Executive Officer and is responsible to the Board of Governors and the Senate for supervision of both the academic and administrative work of the university. This system of governance often makes it difficult for policies regarding sustainability to be adopted, as the academic governance bodies often have completely different agendas than the operations bodies who are often concerned with the bottom line of finances.

Economic barriers are also a key factor affecting change within individual universities. Financial resources within most universities are often scarce. The challenge for those working in the area of sustainability and higher education is to find money in a current climate of fiscal restraint. This is further hindered by what Orr (1995) calls the "business of education"; or the current trend in many Western universities is towards a business model of higher education where students are viewed as clients and where competition is encouraged. In such an atmosphere, short-term thinking seems to supersede long-term vision. Finding monetary support for sustainability initiatives, which might undermine university profits in the short term, but lead to a sustainable future in the long term, can be daunting.

Additionally, although the vast majority of the scientific community feels that sustainability is the key issue that humanity must address in our time, there are others within the academy that disagree and continue to see sustainability as a "fringe" or "special interest" issue. The media seems to perpetuate myths and misconceptions associated with the concept of sustainability, and false notions among those who do not read the academic literature pose an obstacle to pursuing a global sustainability agenda. For example, there exists a concern among many individuals within higher education that sustainability issues have no scientific basis (for example, climate change). Though there is much evidence to the contrary, this lack of public understanding regarding sustainability may remain a significant barrier to creating change in higher education.

Finally, leadership is considered pivotal to ESD. Some schools have seen major results from student grassroots movements toward sustainability; nevertheless, most scholars have expressed that long-term success necessitates the endorsement of ESD from high-level administrators (presidents, provosts, etc.).

A Cause for Hope

Despite the many challenges and barriers, there is evidence of a movement (albeit slow) to reorient higher education toward ESD. A good demonstration of this is the increase in international signatory institutions to the Talloires Declaration from 20 in 1991 to over 357 universities in 2007. This declaration was the first among many international statements made by university administrators of a commitment to sustainability in higher education and remains the best-known declaration in the field. The Declaration states:

> We believe that urgent actions are needed to address these fundamental problems and reverse the trends. Stabilization of human population, adoption of

environmentally sound industrial and agricultural technologies, reforestation, and ecological restoration are crucial elements in creating an equitable and sustainable future for all humankind in harmony with nature. Universities have a major role in education, research, policy formation, and information exchange necessary to make these goals possible (UNESCO, 1990).

The signing of this and other declarations is a wonderful start to creating change, but it is only the beginning. If universities want to fulfill their mandate of solving the complex problems of our time, we must engage in critical reflection of our practice. We must re-think the way we teach, and the way we conduct research. We must think critically about changing the reward system in our university, and re-think the notion of pedagogy. We must determine the university's best role in solving the key problems of our time. Only then will the university truly become a leader in creating a global sustainable future.

References

Brubacher, J. *On the Philosophy of Higher Education.* San Francisco: Jossey-Bass, 1982.

Clover, D., Follen, S., and Hall, B. *The Nature of Transformation: Environmental, Adult and Popular Education.* Toronto: Ontario Institute for Studies in Education, 1998.

Clugston, R. "Introduction." In W. Leal Filho (ed.), *Sustainability and University Life: Environmental Education, Communication and Sustainability.* Berlin: Peter Lang, 1999.

Dewey, J. *On Experience, Nature, and Freedom.* New York: The Liberal Arts Press, 1960.

Filho, L. W. (ed.). Teaching Sustainability—Towards Curriculum Greening. Peter Lang Verlag, Frankfurt, 2002.

Freire, P. *Pedagogy of the Oppressed.* New York: Seabury, 1970.

Mezirow, J. "Transformative Learning: Theory to Practice." In P. Cranton (ed.), *Transformative Learning in Action. New Directions for Adult and Continuing Education.* San Francisco: Jossey-Bass, 1997.

Orr, D. *Earth in Mind.* Washington: Island Press, 1995.

Prescott-Allen, R. *The Wellbeing of Nations: A Country-by-Country Index of Quality of Life and the Environment.* Washington, D.C.: Island Press, 2001.

Scott, J. "The Mission of the University: Medieval to Postmodern Transformations." *Journal of Higher Education,* 2006, 77(1), 1–39.

United Nations Educational, Scientific and Cultural Organization (UNESCO). *The Talloires Declaration.* Gland: UNESCO, 1990.

United Nations Educational, Scientific and Cultural Organization (UNESCO). *Thessaloniki Declaration.* Gland: UNESCO, 1997.

World Commission on Environment and Development (WCED). *Our Common Future.* England: Oxford University Press, 1987.

Wright, T. "Feeling Green: Linking Experiential Learning and University Environmental Education." *Higher Education Perspectives,* 2006, 2(1), 73–90.

TARAH S. A. WRIGHT is an associate professor and Director of Environmental Programmes in the Faculty of Science, Dalhousie University in Halifax, Nova Scotia, Canada.

INDEX